Crack the Code
Finding Answers and Strength in Caring for Aging Parents

Traci Bild

To Sherry Messmer and Chris Andre, through whose care journey I found the courage to write this book.

Table of Contents

INTRODUCTION:	Why This Book Matters	1
CHAPTER 1:	What No One Tells You About Aging Parents	5
CHAPTER 2:	Conversations That Matter	23
CHAPTER 3:	Assembling Your Caregiving Team	34
CHAPTER 4:	When Hospitalization Happens	48
CHAPTER 5:	Navigating the Discharge Process	56
CHAPTER 6:	The Hardest Talk: End-of-Life Wishes & Planning	62
CHAPTER 7:	Understanding Medicare/Medicaid: What's Covered, What's Not	70
CHAPTER 8:	The Puzzle of Medications and Doctors	85
CHAPTER 9:	In-Home Care: Can They Stay at Home?	96
CHAPTER 10:	When Assisted Living is the Next Step	106
CHAPTER 11:	Memory Care and Dementia: The Long Goodbye	117
CHAPTER 12:	Considering Independent Living	128
CHAPTER 13:	The Hidden Costs of Aging	143
CHAPTER 14:	Paying for Care	154
CHAPTER 15:	Final Preparations End-of-Life Care and Hospice	164
CHAPTER 16:	Proactively Preparing for Your Own Journey into Aging	173

Introduction
Why This Book Matters

People often ask me why I live life with such enthusiasm—why I love hosting costume parties, organizing family dinners, traveling as much as I can, or writing handwritten letters to tell people exactly how much they mean to me. The answer is simple: I know how precious life is. I know how quickly it can change.

When he was only 52, I was holding my beloved stepdad, Paul, in my arms, alongside my mother, desperately trying to save him after a massive heart attack. I can still feel the weight of that moment—the heartbreak, the helplessness—as he slipped away from us. A few years later, I found myself in a similar position, saying goodbye to my mother-in-law, Pat, as breast cancer claimed her life far too soon. She was only 57, and she never got to meet her grandchildren. These moments are burned into my memory, and the ages—52 and 57—serve as constant reminders of how fleeting life can be.

These losses changed me. They pushed me to live fully, to appreciate every single day, and to make sure the people I love know exactly how I feel about them while I still have the chance. That's why I take time to write those letters, to host those dinners, and to embrace life with both hands. One day, we will say goodbye to the people we cherish most, and if there's anything loss has taught me, it's that we rarely see it coming.

This is deeply personal for me. But it's also tied to my professional life.

For the last 25 years, I've worked in the senior living and care industry, helping families navigate some of the hardest decisions they'll ever face. I've been part of this field as it's grown from a relatively obscure sector into a vital industry that so many families rely on. Whether it's guiding vibrant seniors into independent living communities or supporting families as they make the painful decision to move a loved one into memory care, my work has been about creating meaningful, compassionate experiences during these pivotal moments.

I've seen the challenges families face firsthand. Whether it's dealing with hospital discharges, trying to understand what Medicare covers, or making the tough decision about assisted living, these are emotional, complicated times for families. I've worked behind the scenes to build services that families can trust, and I've seen how life-changing it is when they have the right support.

My personal experiences, combined with my professional work, have shaped this book. Over the years, friends and colleagues have reached out, desperate for advice on how to handle their aging parents' care. I've seen it time and time again: when a once-strong father starts forgetting names or a once-vibrant mother struggles to get out of bed, families are thrown into crisis. They're overwhelmed, unsure of where to turn, and often unaware of the resources available to them.

That's why I wrote this book.

This isn't just a collection of tips and advice—it's the culmination of both my personal journey and professional expertise. When my own mother's health started to decline, my husband David and I were thrown into a world we knew very little about. Hospital visits became routine, and every six to eight weeks, our lives were turned upside down by another crisis. We had to learn quickly how to advocate for her, navigate a healthcare system that often felt like it was working against us, and figure out how to make sense of the chaos.

I wrote this book so you don't have to stumble through the darkness like we did. I want to give you the knowledge and tools we wished we had from the beginning. This book is here to help you understand your options, ask the right questions, and feel empowered rather than helpless. It's designed to help you navigate the overwhelming process of caring for your aging parents so that what feels like chaos today can become something more manageable.

But more than that, I wrote this book because you deserve to be prepared. You deserve to have the knowledge to fight for your parents, to ensure they live their final years with dignity, love, and the best possible care. You shouldn't be left scrambling in the middle of a crisis, and you don't have to do it alone.

A Personal and Professional Mission

Professionally, I've spent my career helping families like yours. I've seen the difference it makes when families have the right information at their fingertips—when they know about home care options, understand what Medicare and Medicaid cover (and don't), and can access the resources that exist but are often hard to find. I've worked with senior living providers to create trusted communities, places where families can feel supported during these challenging times.

Personally, I've helped countless friends and loved ones through this difficult journey. I've been where you are—feeling lost, scared, and overwhelmed by the unknown. My hope is that this book gives you the roadmap I wish I had, a guide through the emotional, logistical, and financial challenges of caregiving.

This isn't just about surviving the tough moments. It's also about planning for your own future. As hard as it is to think about, we will all face aging one day. Just as you're navigating this journey with your parents now, your children or loved ones may one day face the same with you. By taking control of your future and making your wishes known, you can spare them the heartache, confusion, and overwhelm that you may be experiencing now.

A Final Thought

Caring for aging parents is one of the most emotional, heart-wrenching challenges you will ever face. It's filled with hard decisions, unexpected crises, and moments of deep loss. But it can also be filled with love, connection, and even peace—if you're prepared.

This book is more than a guide; it's a lifeline. It's here to help you navigate the unknown, equip you with the tools you need, and remind you that you are not alone on this journey.

If there's one thing I've learned from my personal losses and professional experience, it's that time is precious. Life is fleeting. But with love, knowledge, and a plan, you can make the most of the time you have—both with your parents and, one day, with your own children.

It's time to take control of this journey. I'm here to help you every step of the way.

Chapter 1

What No One Tells You About Aging Parents

As we reach middle age, certain life realities begin to surface—realities no one truly prepares us for. There's an unspoken transition, a shift in responsibility, and a profound sense of confusion as we watch our strong, independent parents deteriorate. At 54, I, like many others, find myself grappling with a painful dilemma: the challenge of caring for aging parents.

For the past 25 years, I've worked in the senior living sector, witnessing its evolution from a niche field to a critical part of healthcare. Yet despite the growing need for elder care, one glaring truth persists—nobody talks about it. Just as many women don't openly discuss the trials of miscarriage, menopause, or motherhood, we also avoid talking about the difficult reality of caring for our aging parents—a responsibility that overwhelmingly falls on women.

We don't talk about how our roles with our parents will reverse. How the man who was once your strongest ally, mentor, and hero now relies on you to change his diapers, pick him up off the floor when he falls, or comfort him when he forgets your name. Or how your once-vibrant mother will suddenly become a puzzle of ailments, in and out of hospitals, while you and your siblings scramble for answers in a confusing healthcare system that seems to offer more questions than solutions.

I've lived it. My friends are living it. And if you haven't yet, you will.

It's overwhelming. There's no manual to guide you on how to care for the people who once cared for you. Instead, you're left navigating hospitals, home care, insurance, Medicare, assisted living, memory care, and, worst of all, how to pay for it all.

Many adult children find themselves unprepared—scared, confused, and thrown into action with no time to think. The system doesn't help; it's full of hidden services, complex paperwork, and financial burdens that no one warns you about until it's too late.

This book is for you—the overwhelmed, unprepared caregiver trying to navigate your parents' final years. It's a guide to help you plan instead of panic, act instead of react. It's the step-by-step instruction manual you didn't know you needed, but trust me, you will.

Because when the phone rings and it's a hospital, a social worker, or your mother asking for help—this time, you'll be ready.

The Sad Reality: You Are Not Alone

It's important to realize that you are not alone. According to the National Alliance for Caregiving and AARP's 2023 report, Caregiving in the U.S., the number of Americans providing unpaid care has risen to 53 million, up from 43.5 million in 2015. This number will only continue to grow as the population ages. The baby boomer generation, over 70 million strong, is rapidly entering their senior years, and their adult children—like you—are left to manage their evolving and complex needs.

The average caregiver is a 49-year-old woman caring for her 75-year-old mother. She spends about 24 hours a week on caregiving tasks while also managing her own household and career. This "sandwich generation" cares not only for their aging parents but often for their children as well, placing immense emotional, physical, and financial strain on them.

Caregiving impacts every part of your life—your time, your health, and even your career. According to the Caregiving in the U.S. 2020 report, 61% of caregivers are employed. Many reduce their hours or leave the workforce entirely due to caregiving responsibilities. Financially, this can be devastating, especially since caregivers spend an average of $7,000 per year out of pocket for their loved one's care. Caregiving also leads to chronic stress, anxiety, and depression, with caregivers reporting higher levels of physical and mental health issues compared to non-caregivers.

The Dynamics Between Parent and Child: The Unspoken Tension

One of the most challenging aspects of caregiving is the shifting dynamic between parent and child. The emotional toll of watching your once-strong parent become vulnerable, confused, or incapacitated is crushing. It's not just about physical care—it's about grieving the loss of who they once were while adjusting to your new role as their caregiver. This transition often brings unresolved conflicts and emotional exhaustion.

The parent-child relationship is tested in ways you never imagined. Parents may resist care, fearing a loss of independence or not wanting to be a "burden." They may insist they're fine when it's clear they're not. On the other hand, adult children may struggle with guilt—feeling like they aren't doing enough, even when they're doing everything they can.

Caregivers face tough scenarios, including:

- A parent with dementia who becomes aggressive or no longer recognizes them.
- A loved one refusing to move into an assisted living facility, despite it being unsafe for them to remain at home.
- The constant cycle of hospital admissions and discharges, with little support from the healthcare system afterward.

- Disagreements among siblings over caregiving responsibilities or the best course of action.

These situations are common, yet most caregivers are unprepared for the emotional, logistical, and financial challenges they present. The system often leaves them feeling isolated and unsupported.

Lack of Information: Navigating in the Dark

One of the greatest frustrations for caregivers is the lack of clear, accessible information. Whether it's understanding what services are available, navigating Medicare or Medicaid, or simply knowing where to turn for help, caregivers are frequently left in the dark. You may find yourself spending hours on the phone with insurance companies, wading through piles of paperwork, or endlessly searching the internet—only to end up more confused than when you started.

The healthcare system is notoriously difficult to navigate. From unclear hospital discharge plans to inconsistent communication between doctors, caregivers are often left to figure things out on their own. Accessing services like home health aides, physical therapy, or adult day care can feel like a bureaucratic nightmare. Worse yet, many families don't realize the financial burden of long-term care until it's too late. Medicare, for example, covers very little in the way of long-term care, leaving families scrambling to find ways to pay for assisted living or memory care.

A 2021 report from the Insured Retirement Institute (IRI) revealed that only 11% of Baby Boomers have enough savings specifically set aside for long-term care. Even more concerning, 45% of Baby Boomers have no savings at all earmarked for these expenses, despite rising healthcare and long-term care costs. A 2020 report from HealthView Services estimated that the average Baby Boomer couple may need to allocate approximately $387,000 over the course of their retirement for healthcare costs, including long-term care. Yet, most Boomers are unprepared for these expenses, creating a gap between expected costs and actual savings.

The Unspoken Shift: When Roles Reverse

As we age, there's a seismic shift that happens in the relationship between parent and child. The people who once cared for you—feeding you, nurturing you, helping you navigate life—will one day need you to do the same for them. It's a reversal no one really talks about until it happens. One day, your parent is independent and in control of their own life, and the next, they need your help with tasks as basic as remembering to take their medications or getting in and out of bed. It's as if the foundation you once stood on—your parent's strength and stability—has suddenly crumbled, leaving you to hold up the structure of their life.

When Caring for a Spouse

Caring for a spouse brings its own unique and profound challenges. The person who has been your equal partner, your confidant, and your source of strength suddenly becomes the one who relies on you for care. The shared life you've built together—filled with mutual support, love, and shared responsibilities—takes on a new weight as the balance shifts. Where once you both navigated life side by side, you now find yourself shouldering more of the burdens, tending to your spouse's needs with the same love but under vastly different circumstances.

The emotional weight of watching your spouse struggle with daily tasks while managing your own sense of loss can feel overwhelming. It's not just the practical care you're providing—it's the heart-wrenching realization that the person you've shared your life with can no longer stand as your equal. Yet, the love and devotion only deepen, even as the roles shift from partners to caregiver and patient. This change is often unspoken but deeply felt, pulling at both the heartstrings and the foundations of the life you've built together.

What Tends to Happen?

This role reversal can manifest in a variety of ways, often starting with subtle signs:

- Your once-energetic father starts forgetting appointments or repeats the same stories multiple times in a conversation.
- Your mother, always meticulous about her home, starts letting things slide—dishes pile up, bills go unpaid, and personal hygiene becomes less of a priority.
- You notice unexplained bruises on your parents, only to learn they've been falling more frequently but are too proud or embarrassed to admit it.
- Medical visits become more frequent, and your parent starts relying on you to interpret what the doctor is saying or to organize their medication routine.

This shift can feel disorienting for both parent and child. Parents, especially those who have always prided themselves on their independence, often resist this transition fiercely. For them, admitting they need help can feel like losing control of their life—a confrontation with their own mortality. For adult children, the shift can be emotionally overwhelming. Suddenly, you find yourself managing your parent's health, finances, and emotional well-being while balancing your own life, job, and even caring for your own children.

A Story of Love, Distance, and the Hidden Resources for Aging Parents

John had always looked up to his father—a strong, independent man who had spent his entire life in Indiana. His mother, now in her late seventies, had divorced his father 30 years ago and moved to Florida. The two rarely spoke after the divorce, their lives heading in completely different directions. John, the only child who had maintained relationships with both parents, lived across the country in California.

Over the years, John noticed subtle changes in his father's health during their phone calls. His once sharp, witty dad had grown forgetful. Conversations started to repeat themselves, and John began hearing from his father's neighbors about his frequent falls, struggles to maintain the house, and concerning weight loss. It became clear that his father could no longer live on his own.

But John was thousands of miles away, juggling his job, family, and father's growing needs. Despite the distance, he felt responsible for his father's care. The guilt of not being there in person weighed heavily on him. His initial thought was to move his father into a care home in Indiana. But after a few exploratory calls, John realized the costs were astronomical—more than his father could afford and certainly beyond John's financial ability to cover.

In a desperate phone call to his mother, John floated an idea: "Mom, what if we move Dad down to Florida? He could stay with you, and I'd come out as often as I can. I know it's not ideal, but I don't see another option right now." John was already financially supporting his mother, providing her home, and this seemed like the only solution.

After a long pause, his mother agreed. Though they had been divorced for decades, she didn't want to see her ex-husband suffer, and like many women of her generation, she felt a sense of duty to step in.

At first, it seemed like a solution. His father was now in familiar surroundings, and John was comforted knowing his mother could provide basic care. But soon reality set in: his father's needs were more than his elderly mother could manage.

The falls continued. His father couldn't get out of a chair without help and needed assistance with the most intimate aspects of care, including changing diapers and bathing. His mother, still surprisingly active for her age, tried her best. But it became too much. One day, she injured her back while trying to lift him after a fall. The emotional toll was even greater than the physical one—his mother felt overwhelmed and exhausted, struggling with a job she never wanted.

John was beside himself. The guilt of being too far away and the weight of his parents' declining health consumed him. He began researching options, making endless phone calls to local services in Florida, but kept running into dead ends or long waitlists. The local home care agencies were expensive, and private caregivers were beyond their budget. The process felt confusing and isolating.

Then, after months of frustration and near desperation, John came across a lifeline: a publicly funded local aging services organization that provided home care support for seniors at low or no cost. The catch? There was a long waiting list. John immediately added his father's name, and they waited, hoping for some relief.

After several long months, John got the call he had been praying for. His father had been approved for 15 hours of home health care per week. When the home health team arrived for the first visit, they assessed his father's condition and determined that he needed even more support. The care was expanded to 20 hours per week, covered by federal funds channeled through the local agency.

Suddenly, life changed for John, his mother, and his father. Home health aides arrived regularly, helping with the most physically demanding tasks—bathing, changing diapers, and ensuring his father ate nutritious meals. They even made modifications to the home, installing grab bars in the shower and providing medical supplies like diapers and protein shakes. The aides were professional, compassionate, and dependable.

For the first time in nearly a year, John felt like he could breathe again.

His mother, now relieved of the most strenuous caregiving tasks, no longer worried about her own health. And his father, though still declining, was receiving dignified and consistent care from trained professionals.

But John couldn't help but wonder: why had it taken so long to find this service? Why did he have to spend more than a year navigating a maze of confusing information, dead ends, and long waiting periods? And what if he hadn't persisted? What would have happened to his parents if he hadn't found that lifeline in time?

John's story is not unique. Every year, millions of Americans find themselves suddenly responsible for the care of aging parents, overwhelmed by the complexity of navigating services, and unaware of the resources available to them. The information is out there, but it's often hidden behind bureaucratic walls, requiring persistence, time, and, sadly, luck to access.

What If We Knew Sooner?

The truth is, there are incredible resources available to help seniors and their caregivers, but too often, families don't find out about them until they've already been through months—sometimes years—of struggle. John's experience highlights a critical gap in public awareness and access to support systems that could ease the caregiving burden much earlier.

Had John known about the local aging services organization earlier, his father could have received the help he needed long before his mother became overwhelmed. His family's experience could have been drastically different, with less stress, fewer injuries, and more time for emotional connection rather than logistical exhaustion.

The Emotional Impact on Parents and Children

For both parents and their adult children, the role reversal that comes with aging can feel disorienting, painful, and emotionally taxing. The strong, capable parent you've always relied on is now vulnerable, and both of you are forced to adjust to a new normal. This transition doesn't happen overnight, but the emotional impact can be profound.

For parents, the realization that they need help can bring feelings of shame, frustration, and fear. Elderly parents have spent their **entire adult lives being independent**, making their own decisions, running households, and being the backbone of their families. To suddenly become dependent on their children—or anyone else—can be a terrifying experience. The physical decline is bad enough, but for parents, the emotional loss of independence is much worse.

A father who once prided himself on being a strong provider may now find himself needing help getting dressed, using the bathroom, or being lifted out of a chair. This is more than an inconvenience; it feels humiliating, and he may lash out as a result. He might refuse to admit he needs help, insisting he can manage on his own. This often leads to dangerous situations—falls, missed medications, or untreated illnesses—because pride and fear are standing in the way of accepting support.

For an adult child, the emotional burden is equally heavy. Watching your parent decline, both physically and mentally, can feel like you're losing them in slow motion. You may find yourself grieving for the parent they once were, the person who was always there for you and who now no longer seems like the same person. There's the practical frustration of needing to step into a caregiving role while balancing your own life and family. But even harder is the emotional complexity of shifting from being cared for to being the one who provides care.

The Strong Father and the Overwhelmed Daughter

Take Claire, for instance. Her father, George, was the quintessential provider—strong, hardworking, and deeply independent. He never asked for help and was proud of his ability to manage everything on his own. But when his health began to decline, everything changed. George started forgetting to take his medications, and his once-active lifestyle was replaced by days sitting in his recliner, struggling to stand up on his own.

Claire, living just a few towns over, became his primary caregiver. At first, she tried to balance work, her own family, and her father's increasing needs, but she found herself constantly torn between roles. Every visit to his house brought a new wave of grief and frustration—George refused to acknowledge how much help he needed. He insisted he was fine, even when he could barely move without pain. He would become irritable and defensive every time Claire mentioned the idea of home care or assisted living.

Over time, Claire found herself feeling angry and resentful. How could her father be so stubborn? She was exhausted, emotionally and physically, and felt guilty for not doing enough. She missed the relationship they used to have, the easy conversations, and the way he used to protect and guide her. Now, it felt like every interaction was a battle.

The Frail Mother and the Absent Siblings

Susan faced a different kind of challenge. Her mother, Edith, had been declining for years, but Susan was the only one of her siblings who stepped in to help. Edith was frail and needed help with everything from grocery shopping to personal care. Susan's siblings lived far away and rarely visited, leaving her to manage everything alone.

As much as Susan loved her mother, the constant caregiving was overwhelming. She felt abandoned by her siblings and trapped by her responsibilities. Edith, on the other hand, struggled with guilt for being a burden to her daughter. "I don't want to be a problem," she would say, even as she needed help with every daily task.

The emotional toll became unbearable for both—Susan felt isolated and stretched thin, while Edith, embarrassed by her dependence, would often refuse care, making things even harder for Susan.

Coping Strategies: Where to Begin

The emotional complexities of caregiving can't be overestimated, and it's important to recognize that both you and your parent are going through a significant life change. Here's where to start if you find yourself in this position.

Patience and Empathy

Your parent's resistance or frustration is often rooted in fear or shame. Recognizing that this is a vulnerable time for them can help you approach the situation with compassion rather than anger. When they lash out or refuse help, it's rarely about you—it's about their fear of losing control and independence. Keeping this in mind can help you remain patient when frustrations arise.

Set Boundaries for Yourself

While it's natural to want to help your parent as much as possible, you also need to protect your own mental and physical well-being. Setting clear boundaries about what you can and cannot do will help prevent caregiver burnout. It's okay to say no when necessary—it doesn't make you a bad caregiver or child. It makes you human. Overcommitting will only increase resentment and frustration, which will negatively affect both you and your parent.

Involve Professionals Early

Whether it's a geriatric care manager, home health aides, respite care, or exploring senior living options, professionals can help take the burden off your shoulders. Early involvement of outside help can also make the transition smoother for your parent. It allows them to see caregiving as a team effort rather than something that only you, the child, must do.

Lean on a Support Network

Caregiving can feel isolating, but there are support groups and networks that can provide emotional relief and practical advice. Whether it's friends, family members, or online support communities, having people to talk to will help ease the emotional burden. Sharing your struggles and learning from others who are going through the same journey can be a lifeline. As I prepare you for what's ahead, I feel it's important to also share a bit about what your loved one is feeling too because the reality is, this is happening to them and affects their lives even more than ours.

The Senior's Perspective: How I Feel

I don't always say it, but I know you're watching me closely these days. I see the worry in your eyes every time I stumble or forget something. I know you've noticed the little changes—how I move slower, how I need more help with things that used to come naturally. It's hard for me too. I'm trying to come to terms with it, but it's not easy. I never thought I'd need to rely on you the way I do now.

I've always been the one you came to for support. I was the strong one, the one you leaned on when things got tough. And now, here I am, needing help with things as simple as getting out of bed or remembering to take my medication. It's frustrating, and, if I'm being honest, sometimes it's downright terrifying. I don't want to admit that I'm losing control, but I feel it slipping away a little more each day.

I know I can be stubborn—I say I'm fine when I'm not. I insist I don't need help when I clearly do. It's not because I don't appreciate you; it's because I don't want to accept what's happening. I'm scared of losing my independence. It's something I've always prided myself on, and now, needing help feels like I'm losing a part of who I am. I don't want to be a burden on you, even though I know you'd never say that.

It's hard to face the reality that I'm not as strong as I used to be. There are days when I look in the mirror and barely recognize the person staring back at me. And I know it's hard for you too—seeing me like this. I'm sorry for that. I don't mean to make it harder than it has to be, but sometimes the fear and frustration get the better of me. I'm not used to needing anyone like this. And it's hard to admit that I need you now more than ever.

But even though I don't say it enough, I want you to know how much I appreciate everything you do. I see the sacrifices you make—the time you spend here when I know you've got your own family, your own worries. I don't take that lightly. I may not always show it, but every time you help me, I feel your love. And I'm so grateful for that, even if I don't always find the words to say it.

I miss the days when I was the one taking care of you. I miss being the strong one, the person you could count on. Now the roles have changed, and I know it's hard for both of us. But I want you to know that even though I need your help, I'm still your mom. I'm still here, and I still love you more than anything in this world.

I know this isn't easy for you—watching me get older, seeing me struggle. And I'm sorry that you have to carry this burden. But I'm so thankful for you. I hope you know that. I hope you can feel that, even in the moments when I push you away or tell you I don't need help. Deep down, I know I do, and I'm so grateful that you're here for me.

There's something else I need you to know. Even though my body may be failing me, and sometimes my mind feels clouded, I will always be your mother. No matter how much I need you now, that won't change. The love I feel for you is stronger than any of the frustration, the fear, or the loss. And though I may not always say it, every time you're here, helping me through another day, I feel that love reflected back. Thank you—for your patience, your time, and your heart.

Chapter Resources

Here are some valuable support networks for caregivers and seniors, along with their websites. These networks offer a range of emotional, practical, and educational resources for individuals navigating the challenges of aging and caregiving.

- **Family Caregiver Alliance (FCA)**
  - Website: https://www.caregiver.org
  - Support Offered: FCA provides education, support, and advocacy for caregivers of elderly adults. They offer a wealth of resources, including a caregiver support group, webinars, and personalized advice.

- **AARP Caregiving Resource Center**
  - Website: https://www.aarp.org/caregiving
  - Support Offered: AARP's Caregiving Resource Center offers articles, tools, support groups, and online forums where caregivers can connect and share experiences.

- **Eldercare Locator**
  - Website: https://eldercare.acl.gov
  - Support Offered: Eldercare Locator, a public service of the U.S. Administration on Aging, connects older adults and caregivers with local resources, including transportation, home health services, and support groups.

- **Alzheimer's Association**
  - Website: https://www.alz.org
  - Support Offered: The Alzheimer's Association offers support for caregivers and families affected by Alzheimer's and dementia, including online forums, local support groups, and a 24/7 helpline.

- **Caregiver Action Network**
  - Website: https://caregiveraction.org
  - Support Offered: Caregiver Action Network provides free support, education, and resources for family caregivers. They also offer a peer network where caregivers can connect for emotional support.

- **Well Spouse Association**
  - Website: https://wellspouse.org
  - Support Offered: The Well Spouse Association supports spouses and partners of chronically ill or disabled individuals, offering support groups, respite resources, and forums for emotional connection.

- **The National Alliance for Caregiving**
  - Website: https://www.caregiving.org
  - Support Offered: This organization provides research, policy advocacy, and resources for family caregivers. It also connects caregivers with local networks and services.

- **ARCH National Respite Network**
  - Website: https://archrespite.org
  - Support Offered: ARCH helps caregivers find local respite care services, allowing them to take necessary breaks while ensuring their loved ones receive care.

- **Aging Life Care Association (ALCA)**
  - Website: https://www.aginglifecare.org
  - Support Offered: The ALCA connects families with professional aging life care experts (also known as geriatric care managers) who help manage and coordinate care for elderly loved ones.

These resources provide practical help, emotional support, and information for both caregivers and seniors, making the journey of aging or caregiving less isolated and more manageable.

Summary

Caring for aging parents is a journey filled with unknowns and emotional complexity. This chapter unpacks the unspoken truths about the challenges, decisions, and shifts in family dynamics that many face. With understanding and preparation, you'll find ways to navigate these transitions with grace and clarity, knowing you are not alone in this experience.

Chapter 2

Conversations That Matter

"Mom, we need to talk about this."

Sara could feel the weight of the words before they even left her lips. Her mother, once so strong and independent, sat across from her in the living room, surrounded by familiar landscapes of framed photos and keepsakes. The air between them was thick with unspoken fears.

"I know it's hard," Sara continued, her voice cracking, "but we need to talk about what's going to happen if… if something happens to you."

Her mother's eyes softened, but her jaw tightened. "I'm fine, Sara. We don't need to talk about this now."

Sara glanced at her brother, Mark, who had driven in from out of state for this conversation. He sat silently, hands clasped together, avoiding eye contact. They both knew how hard this was for their mother—and for themselves. Talking about the inevitable—the loss, the decisions, the eventual goodbyes—felt like conceding to a reality none of them wanted to face.

But they had to. Sara and Mark had watched too many friends struggle with the chaos that comes from not having these talks, leaving adult children scrambling to make decisions amid grief. They didn't want that for their family. Sara reached out, placing a gentle hand on her mother's knee.

"Mom, we just want to make sure you're cared for in the way you would want."

Her mother sighed deeply, her fingers tracing the arm of her chair. "Alright," she whispered. "Let's talk."

The Importance of Difficult Conversations

Talking to your parents about their care wishes and end-of-life decisions is one of the hardest conversations you'll ever have. It's uncomfortable, emotional, and feels like confronting an inevitable truth. But it's also one of the most important conversations. Without clear communication, families can find themselves in crisis, left to guess what their loved one would have wanted when they are no longer able to speak for themselves.

This conversation must happen *before a* crisis hits, while your parent can still make their own decisions. Avoiding these discussions can lead to confusion, regret, and emotional turmoil. But by approaching the conversation with empathy, patience, and love, you can ensure that your parent's wishes are respected and that your family is prepared for what's to come.

How to Talk to Your Parents About Their Care Wishes and End-of-Life Decisions

Starting this conversation is daunting, but there are ways to ease the tension and encourage openness. Here's a step-by-step guide:

Choose the Right Time and Setting

Timing is everything. Don't bring up these sensitive topics during a rushed phone call or after a medical emergency. Choose a quiet, relaxed setting where you can have an uninterrupted conversation—during a visit, over a meal, or while sitting together at home.

- **Example:** "Mom, I've been thinking about the future, and I'd like to talk about how we can make sure you're taken care of the way you want. Can we find time to discuss this?"

Express Love and Concern

Let your parent know that this conversation comes from a place of love, not fear or pressure. Make it clear that you want to honor their wishes and ensure they're cared for in the best possible way. Frame the conversation as being about them—their preferences, values, and desires.

- **Example:** "I love you so much, and I want to make sure that when the time comes, I'm doing what you want, not guessing."

Start with Open-Ended Questions

Begin with broad, open-ended questions that invite your parent to share their thoughts. This approach prevents them from feeling ambushed or pressured into giving immediate answers.

- **Examples of Starter Questions:**
    - "Have you thought about what kind of care you'd want if you couldn't live at home anymore?"
    - "Who would you trust to make decisions if you weren't able to?"
    - "What medical treatments would you want—or not want—in the future?"

Be Ready for Resistance

It's natural for parents to resist talking about these things. Many don't want to think about their mortality, or they may feel uncomfortable admitting they need help. If your parent resists, don't push too hard.

Reassure them that this conversation is about preventing future stress.

- **Example:** "I know this is difficult, but I want to focus on spending time together later, rather than worrying about paperwork or decisions."

Break It Down into Smaller Conversations

You don't have to cover everything at once. If your parent becomes emotional or overwhelmed, take a break and revisit the conversation later. These discussions can be a series of talks rather than one long conversation.

- **Example:** "We don't need to figure everything out right now. Let's start with what's most important to you."

Listen More Than You Talk

Once the conversation starts, let your parent take the lead. Listen carefully to their thoughts and concerns, offering reassurance that you're there to support their decisions.

- **Example:** "I'm here to listen, and I'll support whatever decisions you make. I just want to be sure I know what's most important to you."

Reassure Them of Their Autonomy

One of the biggest fears for aging parents is losing control over their lives. Reassure your parent that this conversation is about honoring their wishes, not about taking decisions away from them.

- **Example:** "This isn't about taking decisions away from you. It's about making sure we know what you want so we can honor that."

Legal Documents and Conversations to Have Now

While we discussed this in the last chapter, let's dive deeper into these important legal preparations. Having conversations about care wishes is crucial, but it's equally important to formalize them through legal documents. Without these, families can find themselves in a bind.

Key Documents to Have in Place:

1. **Last Will and Testament**
   A will outlines how your parent's assets will be distributed.
   - What to Do: If your parent needs to create or update a will, consult an estate planning attorney. Free or low-cost templates are available online, but legal advice is invaluable.

2. **Durable Power of Attorney (POA)**
   A durable POA appoints someone to make financial decisions if your parent becomes incapacitated.
   - What to Do: Help your parent choose a trusted person and have the document drafted by a lawyer. Ensure it's durable, meaning it remains in effect if they become incapacitated.

3. **Healthcare Power of Attorney and Living Will (Advanced Directive)**
   These documents designate someone to make medical decisions and outline what treatments your parent would or wouldn't want.
   - What to Do: If they haven't done so, find forms through local hospitals or online.

4. **HIPAA Release Form**
   Without a HIPAA release, medical professionals can't share health information with you.
   - What to Do: Ensure this form is signed and submitted to your parent's doctors.

A Tale of Preparedness: How Conversations Can Change Everything

Samantha sat at her mother's bedside, the hum of the hospital room a contrast to the chaos she had feared. Her mother, recently diagnosed with cancer, had complications. But Samantha knew what to do because they'd already had the difficult conversations. They had spent hours discussing care, wishes, and legal documents. Now, in the emergency, she wasn't guessing or panicking.

They had prepared, and that preparation allowed Samantha to focus on being there for her mother, not scrambling through paperwork.

What If You're Already in the Storm?

Samantha's story might feel distant if you're already overwhelmed by caregiving. You may feel like it's too late. But it's never too late to regain control. The difference between chaos and calm isn't about timing—it's about action.

Shifting from Reactive to Proactive—Even in Crisis

Even if you're in the midst of caregiving, you can shift toward a more proactive approach. Here's how:

1. **Begin with Honesty and Transparency**
   Ask your loved one about their wishes moving forward.
   - Starter Question: "I know we're already facing a lot, but can we talk about how you'd like things managed moving forward?"

2. **Focus on What You Can Control**
   Organize medical paperwork, appointments, and other controllable aspects.

- Take Action: Create a binder for critical documents like insurance and medical records.

3. **Seek Professional Help**
   Don't go it alone. A lawyer, geriatric care manager, or therapist can provide support.

4. **Get Legal Documents in Place**
   Even if your loved one's health is declining, getting power of attorney, a living will, and other documents in place can help immensely.

Conclusion
Finding Calm in the Storm

Conversations about care wishes are difficult but necessary to ensure your parent's wishes are honored and to relieve some of the stress on yourself. It's not just about preparing for the worst—it's about empowering both you and your parent to face the future with confidence. Now let's look at what your loved one may be feeling during these conversations.

A Mother's Perspective: What I'm Really Feeling

I know you've been trying to talk to me about this for a while now, and I see the concern in your eyes. But the truth is, I'm scared. I hear your words, and I understand why we need to have this conversation, but every time we start, it feels like we're staring straight at a future I'm not ready to face.

It's hard to talk about these things—what might happen if I can't take care of myself anymore or what I'd want when my time comes. I've spent my whole life being strong for you, for this family, and now

I'm supposed to admit that I won't always be able to do that? It's overwhelming. I don't want to be a burden, and I don't want you to have to make decisions I should be making for myself.

I know you're asking because you love me. You want to be prepared, to make sure everything goes the way I'd want it to. But it's hard to think about needing help like that. I've always been independent—raising you, running a household, living my life on my own terms. The idea of losing that... it feels like losing a part of who I am.

It's not that I don't want to talk about it; I do. It's just that admitting we need to have these conversations makes everything feel so real. And I'm not ready to face the idea that one day I won't be here, or worse, that I might be here but unable to care for myself. It's a fear that sits heavy in my heart, and sometimes it feels easier to avoid it altogether.

But I also know that avoiding it isn't fair to you. I don't want to leave you guessing, not knowing what I'd want when the time comes. I've seen too many friends go through that—struggling to figure out their parent's wishes in the middle of a crisis, left to make impossible decisions on their own. I don't want that for you, and I don't want that for me either.

So, I'll try. I'll push through the fear and the sadness because I know how important this is. I know you're only asking because you love me and because you want to be there for me in the right way. I don't want to make things harder for you when they're already going to be hard enough.

When you ask me what I'd want, it's not that I don't have an answer—it's that saying it out loud makes it feel final. It's like admitting that my time is coming, and that's something I'm not ready to do just yet. But I'll tell you because I trust you, and I know that when the time comes, you'll carry out my wishes with the same love and care you've always shown me.

I hope you know how much I appreciate everything you're doing, even if I don't always show it. I know this isn't easy for you either. Watching your parent get older, facing these hard conversations—it's painful. But I want you to know that I'm proud of you. I'm proud of the way you've handled everything, of the way you've stepped up when I needed you most. I know you're juggling a lot, and I don't take that for granted.

I may not always say it, but I'm grateful. I know I'm not the same as I used to be. I can feel it, just like you can see it. But I'm still your mom, and no matter what happens, I want you to remember that. These conversations are hard, but we'll get through them together, just like we always have.

Additional Chapter Resources:

- **The Conversation Project**
  This initiative is designed to help families have meaningful conversations about care wishes before a health crisis hits. They offer guides to help you start these difficult discussions with your loved ones.
  » **Website**: https://theconversationproject.org

- **Honoring Choices**
  Focused on ensuring that individuals' care preferences are known and honored, Honoring Choices provides resources to help with advance care planning, including healthcare directives and living wills.
  » **Website**: https://www.honoringchoices.org

- **Five Wishes**
  Five Wishes is a national program that helps people write living wills in a more personal and meaningful way. It covers both medical

and personal care wishes, such as spiritual preferences, and offers easy-to-follow instructions.
  - » **Website:** https://fivewishes.org
  - » **Phone:** 1-888-5-WISHES

- **National Hospice and Palliative Care Organization (NHPCO)**
  NHPCO is the largest nonprofit organization that offers education, tools, and resources to help families with end-of-life planning. They provide insight into hospice care and advance care planning.
  - » **Website:** https://www.nhpco.org
  - » **Phone:** 1-800-658-8898

- **Compassion & Choices**
  A nonprofit organization that provides resources to ensure people can make end-of-life care decisions that reflect their values and beliefs. They offer information on advance directives, palliative care, and legal rights related to end-of-life care.
  - » **Website:** https://www.compassionandchoices.org

- **POLST (Physician Orders for Life-Sustaining Treatment)**
  POLST helps ensure that seriously ill or frail individuals receive the medical treatment they want, such as life-sustaining treatments, near the end of life. It complements an advance directive and is recognized across many states.
  - » **Website:** https://polst.org

- **MyDirectives**
  An online platform that allows individuals to create and store their advance care planning documents, including living wills and healthcare powers of attorney.
  - » **Website:** https://mydirectives.com

- **Hospice Foundation of America (HFA)**
  HFA provides information on hospice care, including how and when to start hospice conversations, as well as grief resources for families.
    » **Website:** https://hospicefoundation.org
    » **Phone:** 1-800-854-3402

Chapter 3

Assembling Your Caregiving Team

The moment you realize your parent can no longer care for themselves the way they used to, everything changes. Suddenly, you're thrust into a new role—a caregiver—and it's a heavy responsibility that brings not only logistical challenges but emotional and familial complexities as well. It can feel isolating, overwhelming, and even unfair, especially when family dynamics are involved. Yet, it's crucial to remember that caregiving doesn't have to fall solely on your shoulders. In fact, creating a caregiving team—a group of family members, friends, and professionals—is one of the best ways to navigate this journey.

Caregiving is a collective responsibility, but figuring out how to assemble your team, assign roles, and manage relationships can be fraught with tension. Siblings may disagree on the best course of action, finances often become a point of contention, and even well-meaning family members may struggle to contribute in meaningful ways. Yet, when done thoughtfully, coordinating a caregiving team can transform this difficult experience into something more manageable and even rewarding.

Identifying Family Roles and Responsibilities

When a parent's care becomes necessary, it's common for one sibling to take on the role of the primary caregiver—usually because they live closest or have a more flexible schedule. Statistically, adult daughters are more likely to take on the caregiving role, often juggling full-time jobs, children, and their parent's needs. While this arrangement may seem natural at first, it can quickly lead to resentment if other family members don't share the load, emotionally or financially.

Navigating Family Dynamics

Family caregiving is rife with complexities. Old sibling rivalries, unresolved tensions, and differing opinions on what's best for your parent can bubble to the surface, making an already difficult situation even more emotionally charged. Sometimes, siblings who live far away may feel guilty and either become overly controlling or, conversely, avoid involvement altogether. Others might genuinely want to help but aren't sure how to do so effectively.

A Realistic Look at Responsibilities

Start by having a family meeting—either in person or virtually—where everyone can discuss the situation openly. This is where you define roles, assign responsibilities, and decide on the best plan of care. Here are ways family members can contribute:

- **Primary Caregiver:** This person manages the bulk of day-to-day care—whether that's taking your parent to appointments, managing medications, or assisting with daily tasks. If you're the primary caregiver, be clear about what you can realistically manage and where you'll need help.

- **Financial Manager:** This role involves managing your parent's finances, managing bills, coordinating with insurance, and ensuring that funds are allocated correctly. If one sibling takes on this responsibility, it's crucial they communicate openly with the rest of the family to avoid misunderstandings.

- **Legal Advocate:** Someone needs to manage your parent's legal affairs, including setting up power of attorney, wills, and healthcare directives. This sibling or family member can collaborate with an attorney to ensure that all legal documents are in order.

- **Supportive Caregiver:** Not everyone needs to be hands-on with day-to-day care. Family members can provide emotional support, offer respite to the primary caregiver, or oversee other important tasks like meal preparation, grocery shopping, or home maintenance.

The Sensitive Issue of Finances

One of the most delicate and potentially divisive issues that arise during caregiving is finances. It's not uncommon for siblings to have differing opinions on how to manage the parent's assets, particularly when it comes to selling the family home to pay for care. For example, some siblings may resist selling the house because they see it as their inheritance, while others recognize that using the proceeds to fund assisted living or memory care is in the best interest of their parent.

Advocating for Your Parent

In these situations, it's crucial to remember that the goal is not to preserve the family's financial assets for future generations—it's to ensure your parent gets the best care possible. This can mean selling the home to pay for assisted living or memory care, which often provides a higher quality of life than remaining at home with inadequate support. As the advocate for your parent, you must prioritize their well-being, even when siblings disagree.

When Siblings Disagree

Disagreements over finances or care options can tear families apart. If you and your siblings find yourselves in conflict over these issues, consider bringing in a family mediator or a geriatric care manager. These professionals can help guide the conversation, offer impartial advice, and keep the focus on what's best for your parent, not individual agendas.

Coordinating Support with Siblings and Family Members

Once roles are established, maintaining open lines of communication is essential. A caregiving plan can help keep everyone on the same page and ensure responsibilities are shared fairly. Here are tips for coordinating support:

- **Create a Care Calendar:**
  Use online tools like a shared Google calendar or apps like Lotsa Helping Hands to organize caregiving tasks. This allows family members to see what needs to be done and sign up for specific tasks, ensuring that everyone contributes according to their abilities.
    - Website: https://lotsahelpinghands.com

- **Hold Regular Family Check-ins:**
  Set up monthly or bi-monthly calls to update everyone on your parents' health, any changes in their care, and how the family manages responsibilities. These conversations also provide a chance to air grievances or reassign roles as needed.

- **Stay Flexible:**
  Recognize that roles may shift over time. What worked six months ago may no longer be sustainable as your parent's needs change or as other family members' circumstances evolve.

Professional Help: Knowing When to Bring in Support

As caregiving intensifies, there comes a point when professional help is not only useful but necessary. This can be a difficult realization for both caregivers and families. Primary caregivers feel a sense of duty or guilt, believing they should be able to oversee everything on their own. But caregiving is often too complex and demanding for one person to manage indefinitely. Bringing in professional help is not a failure; it's an act of love and a recognition of your parent's growing needs.

Home Health Aides and Geriatric Care Managers

- **Home Health Aides:** If your parent can still live at home but needs help with activities of daily living (like bathing, dressing, or meal preparation), bringing in a home health aide can be a game-changer. These professionals can assist with physical care while giving you much-needed respite.

- **Geriatric Care Managers:** A geriatric care manager acts as a coordinator and advocate for your parent's care. They help assess your parent's needs, recommend care options, and can even mediate family disagreements. Bringing in a geriatric care manager ensures that your parent receives comprehensive, expert care, and that the pressure is taken off family members trying to navigate the complexities of elder care alone.

- **Aging Life Care Association (ALCA)** - Find local care managers to assist with family caregiving decisions and coordinate care.
    - Website: https://www.aginglifecare.org

Senior Living Options: A Move from Isolation to Community

For many families, there comes a time when it's no longer safe or feasible for a parent to live at home. Senior living options—such as independent living, assisted living, and memory care—become invaluable at this stage.

- **Independent Living:** Ideal for seniors who are still relatively independent but want to live in a community setting where they don't have to worry about home maintenance, cooking, or isolation. Independent living communities often provide social activities, dining options, and amenities like transportation and housekeeping.

- **Assisted Living:** For seniors who need help with daily activities but don't require round-the-clock medical care, assisted living offers a middle ground. Residents have their own apartments but receive assistance with personal care, medications, and other needs.

- **Memory Care:** Specifically designed for individuals with dementia or Alzheimer's, memory care provides a secure environment where trained staff can meet the unique needs of residents. Memory care units often include specialized programs to enhance cognitive function and improve quality of life.

The Benefits of Congregate Living

One of the greatest advantages of senior living communities is the shift from isolation to socialization. Seniors who live alone often experience loneliness, depression, and anxiety. Moving into a senior living community can change all of that. Residents are surrounded by peers, engage in social activities, and form friendships that enrich their lives. They no longer have to worry about cooking, cleaning, or driving—these tasks are handled, allowing them to focus on enjoying their golden years in a supportive, loving environment.

The Financial Reality

Paying for senior living can be challenging. In many cases, selling the family home is the most practical solution. This decision can be difficult for siblings, especially if they view the home as part of their inheritance. However, it's important to remember that your parent's comfort and well-being come first. Assisted living and memory care often provide the care, safety, and social connections that are missing when seniors remain isolated at home. Selling the home can fund years of quality care. Advocating for your parent's needs, even if it causes tension within the family, is the right thing to do.

A Family United: How Assembling a Caregiving Team Changed Everything

The day Melissa received the call from her father's neighbor, her heart sank. Her dad—once the rock of the family—had been found lying on the floor of his home. He had fallen trying to get up from his chair, and hours passed before anyone realized something was wrong. It was a moment Melissa had dreaded but knew would come. Her dad, fiercely independent all his life, had been refusing help, insisting he could handle everything on his own. But now, it was clear his time living alone had ended.

Melissa lived two hours away, juggling a demanding job and raising two teenagers. The weight of her father's care suddenly felt overwhelming, and she knew she couldn't do it alone. Her brother, David, lived across the country and, while supportive, was rarely involved. Like so many adult daughters, Melissa had become the primary caregiver by default.

At first, she tried to manage things on her own. She scheduled doctor's appointments, drove back and forth to her dad's house, and handled his medications. But it quickly became too much. The constant worry for his safety, the late-night phone calls, and trying to balance her family's needs with his care left her exhausted and emotionally drained. She was afraid her father would resist the idea of outside help, but she knew something had to change.

One night, after a particularly concerning health scare, Melissa called a family meeting. She and her brother sat down to discuss their options.

"We can't do this alone," she said, fighting back tears. "Dad needs more help than I can give him. It's not just about us—it's about making sure he's safe and cared for."

David agreed, and together they mapped out a plan. Melissa would remain the primary point of contact, but they decided to hire a geriatric care manager to assess their father's needs and guide them through the process. Despite living far away, David took on managing the finances—paying bills, organizing insurance paperwork, and handling communication with the care manager. For the first time, Melissa felt relief. She no longer had to carry the burden alone.

The care manager, a compassionate and experienced professional, recommended that Melissa's father transition to an assisted living community. Initially, the suggestion felt like a punch to the gut. Melissa had always imagined her dad living out his days at home, where every corner held memories of family dinners and holidays. But the reality was that her father's house was no longer safe. The falls, the isolation, and the strain of maintaining a home were too much.

When they presented the idea to their father, Melissa braced herself for resistance. But something unexpected happened. Instead of fighting the idea, her dad—tired of being alone, struggling with daily tasks, and secretly scared of what would happen if he fell again—agreed.

"I don't want to be a burden," he said softly. "If this is what's best, let's do it."

The transition wasn't easy, but once he moved into the assisted living community, something remarkable happened. Her father, once isolated and lonely, began to thrive. He made friends, joined activities, and started enjoying meals prepared by the community's chefs—no longer worrying about cooking or household chores. He even rekindled his love for playing cards, something he hadn't done in years. For Melissa, it was a revelation. Her father had gone from being isolated and unsafe to part of a vibrant, caring community.

The relief wasn't just emotional—it was practical. With the assistance of the care manager and the community's staff, Melissa no longer had to worry about her father's day-to-day needs. His medications were managed, his meals were taken care of, and she could visit him without the constant stress of caregiving hanging over her. Now, when they sat together, they reminisced about favorite memories or played cards, rather than her rushing around managing his care.

But not everything went smoothly. The decision to sell her father's home to pay for his care wasn't met with the same unity from her brother. David, who had been managing the finances, had hoped to preserve the house as part of their inheritance.

"Are we sure this is the best option?" he asked, hesitating. "I mean, that's the house we grew up in."

Melissa knew it was a tough conversation but understood they had to prioritize their father's needs.

"I get it," she said gently. "I hate the idea of selling it too. But what's more important—Dad having the care he needs or us holding onto the house? He can't live there anymore, David. He needs this community, and selling the house will pay for his care. That's what matters."

After a long pause, David sighed. "You're right. Dad's well-being comes first."

Selling the house was bittersweet, but the financial freedom it provided allowed their father to live comfortably and with dignity. And for Melissa, it meant peace of mind, knowing they had made the right choice, even when it was hard.

Conclusion

Assembling your caregiving team is one of the most important steps you can take to ensure your parent receives the best care while balancing the needs of your family. Identifying roles, setting clear expectations, and bringing in professional support can ease the burden on everyone involved. Remember, this is about your parent's quality of life. Whether through in-home care or a senior living community, the goal is to create a safe, loving environment where your parent can thrive—not just survive.

By advocating for your parent, coordinating with family, and leaning on professional support, you can make the caregiving journey not only manageable but also a time of connection, love, and care that honors your parent's legacy.

A Father's Perspective: What I'm Really Going Through

I've always been proud of my independence. For as long as I can remember, I've handled things on my own—fixing what needed fixing, taking care of my family, and making sure life kept moving forward. But now, things are different. There are days when I can't get up out of the chair without struggling, and it frustrates me more than I can say. I know you see it, too. I can see the worry in your eyes when you visit. I hear it in your voice when you ask if I've taken my medication or if I've been eating enough. I don't want you to worry, but I guess we're past that point.

The idea of needing a "caregiving team" is hard to accept. The truth is, I never wanted anyone to take care of me. It's difficult to admit that I can't handle things like I used to. But I can't deny it anymore—there are too many things I can't do on my own, and it's getting harder to pretend that everything is fine.

I know you're trying to figure out how to make this work, and I appreciate it more than I'll ever be able to say. But it feels strange, doesn't it? You're the ones taking care of me now. And that's not how it's supposed to be. I spent years being the one you leaned on, and now I'm the one who needs help. It's not an easy thing to come to terms with. When you and your brother talked about selling the house, I'll be honest—I didn't like it. This house has so many memories, and I've lived here for so long. It's where I've built my life, raised my family. The idea of leaving it behind, of letting it go—it feels like losing a piece of myself. But I understand why you're bringing it up. It's not safe for me here anymore, no matter how much I want to believe I can still manage. The falls, the isolation ... I know you're right.

But it's hard to let go. It's hard to accept that I can't do this on my own anymore.

When you suggested moving me into an assisted living community, I braced myself. I thought, "This is it. This is the end of the life I've known." But if I'm being honest, part of me was relieved. I've been scared—scared of what might happen if I fall again, scared of being alone. I didn't want to admit that to you because I didn't want to burden you more than I already have. But when you said it might be time for me to move, I realized that maybe it's time to face the truth. I can't keep living like this.

I don't want to be a burden. I've seen the toll it's taken on you, especially with everything else you're juggling. I know you have your own family, your own responsibilities, and I hate the idea that I'm adding more to your plate. That's not what I wanted for you. But I also know you're trying to help me live a better life, and that means more to me than you'll ever know.

I can see how hard it's been for you, trying to manage my care, running around with doctor's appointments, medications, and everything else. I've noticed how tired you are, and that's not fair to you. So maybe, just maybe, moving into a place where I can get the help I need isn't such a bad idea after all.

When you talked about the assisted living community, I didn't expect to feel this sense of relief. At first, I felt like it was giving up, like I was losing everything I'd worked for. But then I thought about it—about the idea of not having to worry anymore. About being surrounded by people, having someone there when I need them. And I realized I don't have to be scared anymore. Maybe this is what I need after all.

I know the decision to sell the house isn't easy for you and your brother. I know David's hesitant, and I understand why. This house is part of our family's history. But you're right. What's more important: holding onto the house or making sure I'm safe and cared for? I hate the idea of selling it, too, but I trust you. I know you're making the decision because you care about me, and that's what matters most.

Moving into the community is going to be a big change. But I have to admit, part of me is looking forward to it. I'm tired of being alone, tired of the quiet, tired of worrying about every little thing. Maybe I'll meet new people. Maybe I'll get to enjoy life again, without the stress of trying to do everything on my own. I've missed playing cards, missed the social side of things. Who knows? Maybe this new chapter of my life won't be so bad.

I want you to know that I'm proud of you—for taking care of me, for stepping up when I need you most. I know this hasn't been easy. I know I haven't made it easy. But I'm grateful for everything you've done, for putting my well-being first, even when it's hard. I may not always show it, but I feel it—your love, your concern, your sacrifices. I don't say it enough, but thank you.

I know things are changing, but I trust you to help me through this. It's not just about making it through—it's about making sure we're still a family, still connected, even as the roles shift. I know you've got my back, and I hope you know that I've always got yours, too.

Additional Chapter Resources for Caregiving Teams

- **Lotsa Helping Hands**
  This free service allows caregivers to coordinate help from family members and friends. The platform provides a shared calendar for tasks, communication tools, and a support network for caregiving families.
  » **Website:** https://lotsahelpinghands.com

- **Caregiver Action Network - Family Caregiver Toolbox**
  The Caregiver Action Network provides tools, resources, and tips to help caregivers navigate family dynamics and caregiving challenges, including managing finances, coordinating care, and seeking professional help.
  » **Website:** https://caregiveraction.org

- **National Institute on Aging (NIA) - Caregiving Resources**
  The National Institute on Aging offers a variety of resources specifically for caregivers, including advice on managing family roles, finances, and finding professional caregiving services.
  » **Website:** https://www.nia.nih.gov/health/caregiving

- **The Caregiver Space**
  This nonprofit provides peer support for caregivers, offering a space to discuss family dynamics, caregiving challenges, and personal stories. It includes online support groups and resources for caregiving teams.
  » **Website:** https://thecaregiverspace.org

- **National Family Caregiver Support Program (NFCSP)**
  This federally funded program offers support to caregivers, including counseling, training, and respite care. It's administered through local Area Agencies on Aging and provides vital resources for families managing caregiving responsibilities.
  » **Website:** https://acl.gov/programs/support-caregivers/national-family-caregiver-support-program

- **ElderCare Resource Planning**
  This service helps families navigate the complex world of eldercare planning, including identifying financial resources, understanding government benefits, and coordinating care teams.
  » **Website:** https://eldercareresourceplanning.org

- **Aging Life Care Association (ALCA)**
  ALCA connects families with certified geriatric care managers who can help with caregiving decisions, assess needs, and coordinate care, which can reduce the emotional and logistical stress on family members.
  » **Website:** https://www.aginglifecare.org

- **National Adult Day Services Association (NADSA)**
  NADSA provides information and resources for adult day care services, which offer professional care and respite to family caregivers. Adult day care services can be a critical support system for primary caregivers while providing high-quality care to seniors.
  » **Website:** https://www.nadsa.org

Chapter 4
WHEN HOSPITALIZATION HAPPENS

It was 2 a.m. when Sarah's phone rang. Her heart sank the moment she saw "hospital" flash on the screen. Her mother, Joan, had been rushed to the emergency room after a fall. In the blur of panic and exhaustion, Sarah made her way to the hospital, where her mother was already admitted. When Sarah arrived, her mother was groggy, hooked up to monitors, and surrounded by nurses. Joan, disoriented and frightened, couldn't remember much about what had happened. Several doctors had already been in and out, but Sarah had missed them all.

A nurse handed Sarah a clipboard with a jumble of notes about medications, tests, and medical history to complete. None of it made sense.

"I wasn't here when the doctors came in. How do I know what's going on?" Sarah asked, feeling overwhelmed and powerless.

"The doctor should be back at some point this afternoon, and you can talk to him then if you are here," the nurse replied kindly before hurrying off to the next patient.

Sarah's mind spun. She had no idea who to speak to, what her rights were, or how to navigate the whirlwind of medical care happening around her mother. Each doctor seemed to offer different information, and Joan, scared and forgetful, couldn't provide clear answers. It felt like trying to solve a puzzle with half the pieces missing.

This scenario is, unfortunately, all too common. When a parent is admitted to the hospital, it can feel like you've lost control, suddenly thrust into a world of medical jargon, doctors coming and going, and an avalanche of paperwork. The experience is not only confusing but emotionally overwhelming. However, you are not powerless. With the right knowledge, you can take control of the situation and ensure that your parent receives the best care possible. What matters is that you demand answers and advocate for your loved one until those answers are provided.

What to Expect and How to Regain Control

Be Present as Much as Possible

The hospital is a fast-moving environment. Doctors make their rounds early in the morning or at unpredictable times, often when family members are not present. Being there when doctors visit can make a big difference in staying informed. If you can't be there physically, ask the nurse to call you when the doctors come by so you can listen via speakerphone. Let the staff know you want to be part of every conversation, even if it's remote.

Tip: If you work or live far away, create a caregiving plan with other family members or close friends. Coordinate shifts so that someone is always present, even if it's not you personally. The more present you or your team are, the more consistent the communication with doctors will be.

Designate a Point of Contact

Hospitals are chaotic, and different specialists—cardiologists, neurologists, surgeons—might all see your parent without clear communication between each other. Ask for a primary point of contact, like the attending physician or a case manager. This person will help you navigate the various medical teams and ensure that all care decisions are coordinated.

Tip: When you first arrive at the hospital, ask the nurse or hospital administrator, "Who is the attending physician for my parent, and when can I speak with them?" Write down their name and make it clear you expect to communicate directly with them about any major decisions.

Keep a Notebook, Digital Record, or Leverage Our Companion Guide

It's easy to feel lost in the flood of information during a hospital stay. Keep a notebook or use your phone to document everything: doctors' names, medications prescribed, tests ordered, and diagnoses discussed. If you don't understand something, ask the doctor or nurse to explain it in simpler terms.

Tip: Ask for a copy of your parent's medical chart daily or request access to the hospital's online patient portal. Many hospitals provide electronic access where you can view test results, medication lists, and doctor notes in real time. Nurses are often very helpful in providing updates and answering questions as well.

Know Your Rights as a Caregiver

You are your parent's advocate. If you have the power of attorney (POA) for healthcare, make sure the hospital has it on file. Without this, doctors may not be legally allowed to share medical information with you. The healthcare POA grants you the right to make decisions on behalf of your parent if they are unable to do so themselves.

Tip: Bring a copy of the POA document to the hospital and present it to the hospital's admissions office. Ask to have it scanned into your parent's medical file. This ensures that every healthcare provider is aware that you are the designated decision-maker.

Ask for a Daily Update

Don't wait for discharge to get a summary of your parent's condition. Request daily updates from the attending physician or nurse. Ask specifically for:
- Results from any tests done that day
- Any changes in medication or treatment plans
- Expected next steps in care (e.g., further tests, consultations with specialists)

Tip: If doctors are discussing treatment options and you feel uncertain, don't hesitate to ask for clarification or time to consider. You can also request a family meeting with all involved specialists to ensure everyone is on the same page.

By following these steps, you can move from feeling disempowered to being an active participant in your parent's care. Hospital stays can be overwhelming, but by staying organized, informed, and proactive, you ensure that your loved one's needs are met.

A Mother's Perspective: What I'm Feeling in the Hospital

Everything is a blur. One moment I was at home, and the next, I'm here—hooked up to machines, nurses coming in and out, people asking me questions I can't seem to answer. I don't even remember how I got here, and that scares me more than anything.

I hate hospitals. They make me feel small and vulnerable, and I don't understand half of what the doctors are saying. I try to follow along, but everything's moving so fast. One doctor comes in, talks for a minute, and then another one follows, saying something different. It's confusing, and I feel completely lost in all of it.

When I saw you walk in, I felt this wave of relief. I've always been the one who took care of things, but now I need you. I'm trying to be strong, but the truth is, I'm scared. I don't know what's going on with my body, and I don't know what's going to happen next. It's overwhelming, and everything feels out of my control.

I see how hard you're trying to get answers, but even when the doctors explain things to you, it feels like they're speaking a different language. I can tell you're frustrated. Believe me, I wish I could help more, but I don't know how. I don't want to burden you with all this, but I don't think I could manage this on my own.

It's hard, too, because I don't want to admit I'm forgetting things, that I can't remember what the doctors just said or what medicines I've been given. It makes me feel weak. And I've always tried to be strong for you. But now, I need you to be the strong one for me, and I'm grateful that you're here. I know you'll ask the right questions, that you'll fight for me when I don't have the energy to do it myself.

I wish I could reassure you that everything's going to be okay, but the truth is, I don't know. I'm trying to trust the doctors, but there's a part of me that just wants to get out of here, go home, and pretend none of this is happening. But I know that's not realistic.

All I can do now is lean on you. And I know that's hard for both of us. I never wanted to be a burden, and I see the toll this is taking on you, too. But knowing you're here, knowing you're by my side, makes me feel like I'm not facing this alone. Thank you for being here, for taking control when I can't. It means more to me than you'll ever know.

National Resources for Hospitalization and Care Advocacy

1. **Patient Advocate Foundation (PAF)**
   PAF offers case management services and resources to help patients and caregivers navigate complex healthcare systems, including hospitalization. They assist with understanding your rights, accessing care, and managing medical bills.
   - Website: https://www.patientadvocate.org
   - Phone: 1-800-532-5274

2. **Caregiver Action Network - Hospital Discharge Planning**
   This organization offers specific resources for caregivers overseeing hospital stays and discharges, providing tips for communication with hospital staff and discharge planning to ensure continuity of care post-hospitalization.
   - Website: https://caregiveraction.org

3. **The Joint Commission - Speak Up™ Initiatives**
   The Joint Commission's Speak Up™ program encourages patients and their caregivers to take an active role in their healthcare, offering resources to ask the right questions and ensure quality care during hospitalizations.
   - Website: https://www.jointcommission.org/resources/for-consumers/speak-up-campaigns

4. **Health Information National Trends Survey (HINTS)**
   HINTS provides information on how patients and caregivers can communicate effectively with healthcare providers, particularly during hospital stays, and how to access patient records and make informed decisions.
   - Website: https://hints.cancer.gov

5. **Hospital Compare (Medicare.gov)**
   Hospital Compare offers detailed information on hospital quality and services, allowing caregivers to evaluate the performance of hospitals, compare their safety ratings, and better understand the care their loved one may receive.
   - Website: https://www.medicare.gov/care-compare/

6. **American Hospital Association (AHA) - Caregiver Resources**
   AHA provides tools for caregivers, including guidelines on interacting with hospital staff, managing patient rights, and preparing for hospital stays.
   - Website: https://www.aha.org

7. **National Patient Advocate Foundation (NPAF)**
   NPAF is a nonprofit organization that focuses on ensuring patient and caregiver voices are heard in healthcare settings. They offer resources to help families understand their rights during hospitalization and how to advocate for their loved ones.
   - Website: https://www.npaf.org

Summary

A sudden hospitalization can be a turning point for your aging parent's care. This chapter guides you through advocating for your loved one, asking the right questions, and preparing for what comes next. Armed with these insights, you'll be better equipped to manage the stress and uncertainty of medical emergencies.

Chapter 5

Navigating the Discharge Process

A few days after Joan's hospitalization, Sarah received a call from the hospital. Her mother was being discharged tomorrow. Relief washed over her—until the realization hit. What now? How could her mother, still weak and recovering, be ready to go home? What if something went wrong once they left the hospital?

Discharge can often feel like stepping off a cliff with no safety net. Hospitals are under pressure to free up beds, so patients are sometimes discharged too early or without proper instructions. Without clear guidance, families are left scrambling to figure out the next steps, often with little support. But you can prevent this by knowing what to ask and preparing ahead of time.

Questions to Ask Before Discharge

Is My Parent Truly Ready to Go Home?

Before agreeing to a discharge, ask the medical team if they believe your parent is truly ready. If your loved one is still frail or struggling with basic activities, question whether they might stay another day or be better served in a rehabilitation facility first, where they can receive round-the-clock care for a few more days or weeks.

Tip: If you're not comfortable with the discharge plan, speak up. Ask for a detailed assessment of your parent's mobility, ability to manage medications, and overall readiness to return home. You have the right to request a rehabilitation stay if it seems necessary. Do not let your parent be discharged if you feel it's unsafe to do so.

What Specific Care Will Be Needed at Home?

Get a written care plan that includes instructions for at-home care. This should cover:

- **Medications:** What to take, when, and any side effects to watch for.
- **Wound or incision care:** If your parent had surgery or an injury, make sure you understand how to care for wounds or incisions properly.
- **Mobility assistance:** Will your parent need help getting in and out of bed, using the bathroom, or walking? Ask if medical equipment, like walkers or shower chairs, will be provided.
- **Help with daily living:** If your parent needs help with bathing, dressing, or meal preparation, ask if home health aides can be provided. Many times, this is covered under Medicare or private insurance, but you may need to ask for it specifically.

What Follow-Up Appointments Are Required?

Before discharge, make sure any follow-up appointments are scheduled. Whether your parent needs to see a primary care physician, a specialist, or a physical therapist, get clear dates and contact information. Make sure these appointments are booked before leaving the hospital if possible.

What Red Flags Should I Watch For?

Ask what symptoms or changes in condition would signal an emergency. Should you watch for fever, increased pain, or signs of infection? Knowing what's normal and what requires immediate attention can save you from panic later. If your parent is weak, unable to walk, or experiencing other visible concerns, be sure to refuse discharge orders until you feel it is safe or a post-hospital stay care plan is in place. Depending on hospital bed demand, it's possible to be discharged too early to make room for a new patient.

Are There Support Services We Can Access?

Many hospitals partner with local services to provide post-hospitalization support, such as meal deliveries, transportation to follow-up appointments, or at-home health services. Ask about these resources, and don't leave until you know what's available.

By asking these key questions, you can ensure that your parent's transition home is as safe and smooth as possible. Discharge shouldn't feel rushed or incomplete—your loved one deserves a thoughtful, well-planned return home.

A Mother's Perspective: What I'm Feeling During Discharge

They're telling me it's time to go home tomorrow. I should be relieved, I guess. After all, I've never liked hospitals—the constant noise, the poking and prodding. But right now, all I can feel is this pit of anxiety in my stomach. Am I really ready to go? It feels too soon. I'm still weak; my body isn't moving the way it used to, and honestly, I'm scared.

I know you're doing your best to figure out what's next, but I can tell you're just as worried as I am. We've both been here before—doctors say it's time to go, but what happens when I walk through the front door at home? I don't even know if I can walk without help, let alone manage all the other things that come with day-to-day life.

What if I fall again? What if something goes wrong? The idea of going home used to be comforting, but now it feels like stepping into the unknown, without the nurses or doctors just down the hall. And I can see it on your face—you're asking questions, trying to get answers, but I know neither of us really knows what to expect.

I don't want to be a burden. I don't want you worrying about me every minute, wondering if I'm okay when you're not around. I want to tell you I'll manage, that I can do this, but I'm not sure I can. And I hate admitting that. I hate feeling so vulnerable, so dependent. I know you're tired—you've been by my side, taking on more than you should have to, and now the idea of all this responsibility following us home ... it's overwhelming.

But what choice do we have? The hospital says it's time. They've got other patients waiting, and I know I'm not their only concern. But I need to be sure that when we leave here, I'll be safe. I need to know what happens next—how I'm supposed to manage at home. How are we going to handle medications, appointments, just getting around the house?

It feels like they're rushing us out the door, like we're expected to just figure it out on our own. But I'm not the same as I was before this happened. I need help, real help, not just a few scribbled instructions on a piece of paper. I can't tell you how much it means to me that you're here, asking all the right questions, trying to make sure I'll be okay once we leave. But I wish someone would sit down with us and explain it all clearly—what I'm supposed to do, what you're supposed to do. Because right now, I feel like we're walking into this blind.

I need to know that you won't be alone in this, too. It's not fair for you to carry all of this by yourself. I see the weight you've been carrying, and I don't want to add to it. We need a plan—something solid, something that gives both of us some peace of mind.

So before we walk out of here, I hope we get the answers we need. I need to know that you're not going to be left scrambling, that there will be people helping us once we're home. I don't want to end up right back in the hospital because we weren't prepared. I just want to feel safe again.

I may not say it enough, but I trust you to figure this out. You've been my rock through all of this, and I know you're doing everything you can. I'm scared, but having you by my side makes it a little easier. Just promise me one thing: if we don't feel ready, if you're not sure it's safe, you'll speak up. Don't let them rush us if it doesn't feel right. I need you to be my voice, especially when I'm too tired to fight.

National Resources for Navigating the Discharge Process

1. **Care Transitions Program**
   The Care Transitions Program offers tools and guidance to help patients and caregivers manage the transition from hospital to home. The program emphasizes coaching and collaboration between caregivers and healthcare professionals to reduce hospital readmissions and improve post-discharge outcomes.
   » **Website:** caretransitions.org

2. **Home Health Compare (Medicare.gov)**
   This tool from Medicare helps families find and compare home health care agencies based on the quality of care they provide. It can be especially useful when arranging home health services after discharge.
   » **Website:** https://www.medicare.gov/care-compare/

3. **National Transitions of Care Coalition (NTOCC)**
   NTOCC is a nonprofit organization dedicated to improving the quality of care transitions, such as moving from the hospital to home or a rehabilitation center. Their resources help caregivers understand how to ensure proper continuity of care and avoid common pitfalls of the discharge process.
   » **Website:** ntocc.org

4. **Hospital Discharge Planning: A Guide for Families and Caregivers (CMS)**
   The Centers for Medicare & Medicaid Services (CMS) offers a comprehensive guide specifically for caregivers navigating the discharge process. It provides practical information on coordinating care and ensuring all necessary services are in place before discharge.
   » **Website:** medicare.gov/publications

5. **Discharge Planning Toolkit (Family Caregiver Alliance)**
   Family Caregiver Alliance provides a discharge planning toolkit that helps caregivers ensure they have the necessary information and support when a loved one is released from the hospital. It covers everything from medication management to follow-up care and support services.
   » **Website:** caregiver.org

6. **Hospital Patient Rights (American Hospital Association)**
   The AHA outlines patient rights regarding discharge, including how to appeal a discharge if you feel your parent is being released too early. This resource explains the discharge appeal process and patient rights during hospitalization.
   » **Website:** aha.org/advocacy/patient-bill-rights

7. **Community Health Accreditation Partner (CHAP)**
   CHAP provides accreditation for home health care and hospice services. Caregivers can use CHAP's directory to find accredited home health services to ensure quality care after discharge.
   » **Website:** chapinc.org

Chapter 6
The Hardest Talk: End-of-Life Wishes & Planning

When it became clear that her father's health was declining, Megan dreaded the conversation she knew was coming. How could she ask him about his wishes for the end of his life? Every time she thought about bringing it up, she felt paralyzed. But as his hospital visits became more frequent, she realized that without knowing his wishes, they'd soon face difficult decisions without his guidance. The conversation couldn't wait any longer.

Like Megan, many caregivers struggle to have important conversations with their aging parents about their care needs and end-of-life decisions. It's understandable—these conversations are emotionally charged, and no one is ever truly prepared to talk about the implications of aging. Yet, these discussions are essential. By talking openly with your parent about their care preferences, legal documents, and long-term plans, you can ensure their wishes are honored and prevent unnecessary stress down the line.

In this chapter, we'll walk through how to approach these difficult conversations with empathy and care, provide practical advice on what to discuss, and emphasize why having these conversations sooner rather than later can lead to peace of mind for both you and your loved one.

Expanding on Emotional Struggles: Why These Conversations Feel So Hard

It's no surprise that talking about end-of-life decisions with a parent can feel impossible. These discussions force both you and your loved one to confront uncomfortable realities—aging, loss of independence, and eventually, death. For parents, the idea of giving up control or facing their mortality can lead to resistance. They might avoid the topic, dismiss your concerns, or insist that they are fine.

As a caregiver, you may feel just as resistant to having these conversations. You don't want to upset your parent, and you may feel guilty for bringing up such a sensitive subject. Yet, delaying these conversations only increases the emotional burden for both of you when a health crisis eventually forces the issue.

The key to navigating these discussions is approaching them with empathy and a clear intention of love and support. Acknowledge how difficult the conversation is for both of you but frame it to ensure their wishes are respected and that they have a voice in the decisions being made about their care.

Practical Tips for Starting These Conversations

So, how do you begin these conversations? Here are some tips to help you approach the topic in a way that's loving, respectful, and productive:

Choose the Right Time

Don't wait for a crisis to have these discussions. Instead, choose a calm, stress-free moment when you and your parent can talk openly. It's better to approach the topic over a quiet dinner or during a family gathering when everyone is relaxed.

Start Small and Gradual

You don't have to cover everything in one conversation. Start by asking how they're feeling about their health or whether they've thought about what they want their future to look like as they get older. Let the conversation unfold naturally over time, rather than overwhelming them with too many questions at once.

- **Opening Statement:** "Dad, I've been thinking a lot about your health lately, and I want to make sure we're both on the same page about what you want in the future. I know it's not an easy topic, but I'd love to talk about how we can make sure you get the care you want."

Use Examples from Others' Experiences

If your parent is hesitant, you might gently bring up stories from other families who faced difficult decisions without knowing their loved one's wishes. This can help them see the importance of having a plan in place.

- **Example:** "I remember how hard it was for Aunt Beth when Grandpa got sick and they didn't know what kind of care he wanted. I don't want us to be in that situation. I think it would give us both peace of mind if we talked about it now."

Acknowledge Their Fears

Listen to their concerns without interrupting. If they express fears about losing control or giving up their independence, validate those feelings and reassure them that the goal is to make sure their preferences are respected.

How These Conversations Can Change Everything

Once you've started these conversations, you'll be amazed at the sense of relief that often follows. By proactively talking about your parent's wishes—whether it's their preferences for medical care, living arrangements, or how they want to be remembered—you are not only helping them take control of their future but also giving yourself a roadmap for what lies ahead.

When Megan finally had the conversation with her father, it was tough, but it led to important decisions. They talked about living wills, healthcare proxies, and what he wanted in terms of life support or resuscitation. The conversation didn't end in sadness—it gave them both a sense of peace. Afterward, her father seemed relieved, knowing that his wishes would be honored, and Megan felt empowered by the knowledge that she wouldn't be left guessing in a crisis.

These discussions may be difficult, but they are also acts of love. They ensure that when the time comes, you can focus on caring for your loved one rather than scrambling to figure out what they would have wanted.

Honoring the Legacy of Communication

Talking about aging, care needs, and death isn't just about logistics—it's about honoring your parent's legacy and giving them the opportunity to make their voice heard. These conversations allow your parent to feel empowered, involved, and respected. And when the time comes to make hard decisions, you can do so with confidence, knowing you are fulfilling their wishes.

Conclusion

While the thought of having these conversations may fill you with dread, the peace of mind that follows is worth every difficult moment. Approach these discussions with patience, compassion, and honesty, and remember that these are conversations born out of love. Your parent has taken care of you for much of your life—now, it's your turn to ensure that they are cared for in the way they deserve. When the time comes, you'll be grateful that you both took the time to talk openly about what matters most.

A Father's Perspective: Facing the Tough Conversations

I've always prided myself on being able to handle things. I've been through my share of ups and downs, and no matter what, I found a way to take care of myself and my family. But lately, things have been different. My body doesn't seem to listen to me the way it used to, and I can tell by the way you look at me that you're worried. I can see it in your eyes—the questions you want to ask but don't. I know what's coming.

You're thinking about the future, about what happens when I'm not as strong as I used to be. And I get it—I've been thinking about it too. But the truth is, I don't want to talk about it. It feels too final, too real. I don't want to admit that I'm getting older, that there might come a time when I can't make decisions for myself. And I sure don't want to think about the end.

Still, I know this conversation needs to happen. I can see that you're struggling to bring it up, and I don't want to make it harder for you. You're only trying to make sure I'm taken care of, to understand what I want when the time comes. I'm not angry with you for asking—I'm just scared. Talking about these things feels like giving up control, like acknowledging that there's a point when I won't be the one calling the shots anymore. And that's a tough pill to swallow.

But when you finally do bring it up, in that gentle way of yours, I realize that maybe this conversation isn't as bad as I thought. You're not trying to take anything away from me—you're trying to make sure I have a say. You want to know what I want, so when the time comes, you won't have to guess. And deep down, I appreciate that. You're showing me the same love and care I tried to show you all those years.

I know you're afraid of upsetting me, and believe me, part of me wants to brush it off, say I'm fine, and not worry about it. But I also don't want you to be left in the dark when things get tough. I don't want you to have to make those big decisions without knowing what I would have wanted. You deserve better than that—you've always been there for me, and the least I can do is make sure you know where I stand.

When you bring up those stories about other families, how they had to make hard choices without knowing what their parents wanted, I feel a pit in my stomach. I don't want that for us. I don't want you to go through that uncertainty, wondering if you're doing the right thing. So, as hard as this conversation is, I know it's the right thing to do.

We start small, like you suggested, and somehow, it's not as overwhelming as I feared. You ask about my health, what I'd want if things took a turn. You tell me how much you care, that you just want to make sure I'm comfortable, that I'm taken care of the way I deserve. And slowly, I begin to open up. We talk about what I'd want if I couldn't make decisions for myself. I tell you my thoughts on life support, resuscitation, and all those things I didn't want to think about before. It's not easy, but it feels good to finally get it out in the open.

In some strange way, I feel a little lighter after we talk. It's as if a weight I didn't even know I was carrying has been lifted. I see the relief in your eyes, too—now you won't have to worry about not knowing what to do when the time comes. And that gives me peace.

This conversation, as tough as it was, has brought us closer. It's given me a sense of control over what happens next, even if I'm not around to make those decisions. I want you to know that when the time comes, I trust you. I trust that you'll make sure my wishes are honored, that you'll be there for me, just like I've always tried to be there for you.

I may not say it often, but I'm proud of you. You've taken on so much already, and I'm grateful that you care enough to have this difficult talk with me. I know it's not easy for either of us, but we got through it. And now, when the time comes—whenever that may be—you'll know what I want, and we'll both have a little more peace because of it.

National Resources for End-of-Life Conversations and Planning

1. **The National Hospice and Palliative Care Organization (NHPCO) - CaringInfo**
   NHPCO's CaringInfo provides free resources and information to help families have conversations about advance care planning and end-of-life decisions. Their guides help with discussions about hospice, palliative care, and documenting care preferences.
   » **Website:** caringinfo.org
   » **Phone:** 1-800-658-8898

2. **Death Over Dinner**
   This initiative encourages families to come together and have conversations about end-of-life care over a meal. It provides conversation starters, resources, and tools to help families discuss topics like living wills, healthcare proxies, and other end-of-life decisions in a casual, supportive setting.
   » **Website:** deathoverdinner.org

3. **Prepare for Your Care**
   Prepare for Your Care is an online resource that guides families through the process of having end-of-life conversations. The site provides easy-to-understand information about advanced directives, medical decision-making, and how to communicate your wishes effectively.
   » **Website:** prepareforyourcare.org

4. **Respecting Choices**
   Respecting Choices offers tools for advance care planning that focus

CRACK THE CODE

on person-centered care. They provide resources to help individuals and families create and share their advanced directives and have meaningful conversations about their healthcare wishes.
- » **Website:** respectingchoices.org

5. **End-of-Life Planning Checklist (Hospice Foundation of America)**
Hospice Foundation of America provides a detailed checklist to guide families through end-of-life planning discussions. The checklist covers legal documents, healthcare preferences, and burial or memorial wishes, making the conversation more manageable.
   - » **Website:** hospicefoundation.org

6. **GoWish Cards**
GoWish Cards are a practical tool designed to facilitate discussions about end-of-life care preferences. The cards are used as conversation starters to help people and their families prioritize what matters most to them regarding medical treatment, comfort, and quality of life.
   - » **Website:** gowish.com

7. **Aging With Dignity - Five Wishes**
Five Wishes is a widely used advance directive that helps people document their end-of-life wishes in a simple, user-friendly format. It covers medical, emotional, and spiritual aspects of care and provides a clear path for families to honor their loved ones' wishes.
   - » **Website:** fivewishes.org
   - » **Phone:** 1-888-5-WISHES

Chapter 7

Understanding Medicare/Medicaid What's Covered, What's Not

When Sarah's mother, Joan, first turned 65, they both felt reassured knowing that Medicare would now cover most of Joan's medical needs. It seemed like a safety net, a promise fulfilled after years of working and paying into the system. For a while, it worked as expected—doctor visits, hospital stays, and medications were covered. But as Joan's health began to decline, that safety net started to fray. She needed help with basic daily activities like bathing and dressing, and then came the crushing diagnosis of Alzheimer's.

Suddenly, Sarah was faced with the staggering costs of long-term care that Medicare simply didn't cover.

Like many caregivers, Sarah was shocked to discover that Medicare, while essential for many medical needs, doesn't cover long-term care—the kind of care that aging parents like Joan need most as their health deteriorates. After months of research and frustration, Sarah learned that Joan could receive in-home physical therapy, occupational therapy, and even help with bathing and dressing—all covered by Medicare. But by then, Joan's modest savings had already begun to drain, and Sarah faced the harsh reality that her mother would need to spend down her assets to qualify for Medicaid to afford the skilled care she desperately needed.

This is a story many families know too well. Navigating Medicare and Medicaid can be incredibly confusing, especially for those new to caregiving. But understanding these programs—and what they cover—

can make the difference between your loved one receiving the care they need or struggling through a system that seems indifferent to their needs.

What Type of Medicare Does My Parent Have?

The first step in navigating this complex system is understanding the type of Medicare your parent has. Medicare is not a one-size-fits-all program, and it comes in several parts:

- **Medicare Part A:** Covers hospital stays, skilled nursing care (after a hospital stay of three or more days), and some home health services.
- **Medicare Part B:** Covers doctor visits, outpatient care, medical equipment, and some preventive services.
- **Medicare Part C (Medicare Advantage):** These are private plans approved by Medicare that may offer additional coverage, such as dental or vision care, with different rules about hospital stays and follow-up care.
- **Medicare Part D:** Covers prescription drugs.

To find out what type of Medicare your parent has, you can check their Medicare card, log into **Medicare.gov,** or call 1-800-MEDICARE for assistance.

Ensuring You Have Access to Information

If your parent is unable to manage their Medicare or healthcare information, you'll need to have a Healthcare Power of Attorney (POA) in place to speak with doctors and insurance providers on their behalf. Here's how to ensure you can access your parent's medical information and manage their care:

- **Ensure the Power of Attorney is in Place:**
  If you haven't already done so, work with an attorney to create

a Healthcare Power of Attorney. This document must be signed by your parent while they are still mentally capable of making decisions.

- **Submit POA to Medicare and the Hospital:**
  Once you have the POA, bring a copy to the hospital and submit a copy to Medicare. You can do this by contacting Medicare and filling out their Authorization to Disclose Personal Health Information form.

What's Covered Under Medicare?

Understanding what Medicare does—and does not—cover can help you avoid surprises and unnecessary stress. Here are some key services covered by Medicare:

- **Hospital Stays and Rehab:**
  Medicare Part A covers inpatient hospital care and rehab stays in skilled nursing facilities, but there are limits. For example, after 20 days in a skilled nursing facility, you may have to pay part of the costs. Ask the hospital how long Medicare will cover your parent's stay and what happens after that period ends.

- **Home Health Care:**
  If your parent qualifies, Medicare Part A may cover home health services, including:
    - Nursing care
    - Physical or occupational therapy
    - Help with bathing and dressing
    - Medical equipment, like walkers or hospital beds

  Tip: You may need to specifically ask for these services—hospitals don't always proactively offer them.

- **Medications:**
  Under Medicare Part B and Part D, some medications are covered during hospital stays and post-discharge. Be sure to ask the doctor or pharmacist which medications are covered and if there are any additional prescriptions you'll need to purchase.

Medicaid: A Different Set of Benefits

Medicaid is often the next step when Medicare falls short, especially for long-term care. If your parent qualifies for Medicaid, the coverage expands to include long-term care options that Medicare doesn't cover. This includes:

- Nursing home care (for long-term stays)
- Personal care aides to help with daily living tasks
- Adult day care programs that provide social and health services during the day

If your parent is on Medicaid, work closely with the hospital social worker to ensure you're accessing the full range of benefits. Ask questions to make sure your loved one receives all benefits available to them, as they will not always be offered proactively.

Why Someone Moves from Medicare to Medicaid

Medicare and Medicaid serve different purposes, but when it comes to long-term care, most families eventually must rely on Medicaid. Medicare, while covering many short-term medical needs, doesn't cover the kind of long-term care required for conditions like dementia, Alzheimer's, or physical disabilities. Sadly, senior living, such as assisted living and memory care, is not covered by Medicare or Medicaid. As of the writing of this book, these options are 100% private pay.

Medicaid, on the other hand, is designed for people with low income and limited resources. It offers a broader range of services, such as skilled nursing care, home health aides, and long-term care facilities. However, to qualify for Medicaid, an individual must meet strict income and asset limits.

Understanding the Spend-Down Process

The spend-down process requires individuals to reduce their assets to a level where they meet Medicaid's eligibility requirements. In most states, an individual can have no more than $2,000 to $3,000 in assets (with some exemptions, like a primary residence or car) to qualify. Here's how the process works.

Liquidating Assets:

If your parent has savings, investments, or property, these assets often must be used to pay for care until their financial resources are depleted. This might mean using retirement funds or selling the family home to cover the cost of a nursing home or in-home care.

Using Savings for Care:

For someone like Joan, who required skilled nursing care for Alzheimer's, costs in a facility could reach $8,000 per month or more. Medicare might cover the first 20 days in a skilled nursing facility, but after that, most costs fall on the family unless long-term care insurance is in place (which many people do not have). Joan's savings, intended for retirement and emergencies, were quickly drained.

Becoming Medicaid-Eligible:

Once an individual's assets are spent down to the required level, they can apply for Medicaid. At that point, Medicaid steps in to cover the cost of skilled nursing care or in-home support, ensuring the person receives the care they need for the rest of their life.

A Heartbreaking Reality

The transition from Medicare to Medicaid is often filled with emotional and financial conflict. Families must confront the harsh reality that, for their loved one to receive the care they need, they may have to sacrifice everything they've worked for. For many, this means selling the family home—a place filled with memories and sentimental value.

It's difficult to watch a parent's life savings disappear to cover the cost of care. The sense of injustice—knowing they worked hard their entire lives, only to spend their final years in financial ruin—can be overwhelming. Yet for many families, Medicaid is a lifeline, offering access to care that would otherwise be unaffordable.

Understanding the spend-down process and Medicaid eligibility is crucial for caregivers, as it allows families to plan ahead. Here are a few steps to prepare:

Consult an Elder Care Attorney:

An elder care attorney can help you navigate Medicaid eligibility rules in your state and guide you through the spend-down process. There are strategies, such as Medicaid asset protection trusts, that may allow your parent to preserve some assets while still qualifying for Medicaid. The earlier you seek advice, the better you can plan.

Prepare for Hard Conversations:

If your parent is still healthy, start discussing their long-term care preferences now. These talks are difficult, but they allow your parent to express their wishes before a crisis forces decisions.

Know What Medicaid Covers:

Once your parent qualifies for Medicaid, it's important to understand what services are covered. Medicaid provides nursing home stays, home health aides, and adult day care services.

A Story of Navigating the Medicare-to-Medicaid Transition

Emily's heart sank as she stared at the hospital discharge papers in her hand. Her father, Jack, was being sent home after a two-week stay following a fall that had broken his hip. Emily had been by his side every day, listening to the doctors, taking notes, and asking questions. But now, as she prepared to bring him home, she was terrified. Jack was no longer the strong, independent man she had always known. At 78, his body was fragile, and his memory was slipping. He needed help with everything—bathing, dressing, eating—and Emily wasn't sure how they would manage.

As Jack's only child, Emily felt the weight of responsibility, but she was already stretched thin. She had a demanding job, a new grandbaby she watched during the week, and her own health challenges. On the way home from the hospital, questions began swirling in her mind. How would they pay for help at home? How long would Medicare cover his physical therapy? Would he need to go into a nursing home? And how on earth would they afford that?

Starting with Medicare

When Jack first turned 65, Medicare had been a blessing. It covered his doctor's visits, medications, and occasional hospital stays. Emily had been relieved, thinking Medicare would take care of him as he aged. But now, as Jack needed long-term care, Emily realized just how much

Medicare didn't cover. It would pay for a limited number of days in a skilled nursing facility after his hospital stay, but beyond that, she was on her own.

During the first few weeks at home, Jack had in-home physical therapy paid for by Medicare, and a nurse came by to check on him a few times a week. But it wasn't enough. Jack needed help with daily living—bathing, dressing, meals—and Medicare didn't cover those services. As Emily started searching for more help, the reality of how expensive long-term care would be began to sink in.

The Financial Burden of Long-Term Care

Emily quickly realized the cost of caring for Jack at home, or placing him in a facility, was staggering. Even a part-time home health aide would cost thousands of dollars a month, and a full-time aide or a nursing home would cost even more. Jack's savings were modest—he had worked hard his whole life, but there wasn't enough to cover the level of care he needed for the long term. Emily knew it wouldn't be long before his money ran out.

That's when she learned about the spend-down process. To qualify for Medicaid, Jack would have to reduce his assets to below a certain threshold, leaving him with just a few thousand dollars. Emily sat with her father as they went over his finances. It was heartbreaking. Jack had been proud of the small nest egg he had built, and now he would have to spend it all just to get the care he needed.

"Why did I work so hard if it's all going to be gone anyway?" Jack asked, his voice trembling. Emily didn't have an answer. All she could do was hold his hand and promise she would make sure he was cared for, no matter what.

Transitioning from Medicare to Medicaid

With the help of an elder care attorney, Emily began the process of spending down Jack's assets. They sold his car, liquidated some investments, and used his savings to pay for a few months of home care. It was painful watching Jack lose the financial security he had worked his entire life to build.

Once Jack's assets were low enough, Emily applied for Medicaid on his behalf. It was a long and confusing process—filling out forms, gathering financial documents, and waiting for approval. But finally, after weeks of paperwork and phone calls, Jack was approved for Medicaid. Now, his care would be covered, and he could stay in a nursing home that offered round-the-clock assistance. Still, the emotional toll of the process weighed heavily on both of them.

The Emotional Toll of Letting Go

The day Emily helped move her father into the nursing home was one of the hardest of her life. She had grown up in their family home, and it was full of memories—birthday parties, holidays, and quiet evenings spent with Jack after her mother passed away. Selling the house had been part of the spend-down, and now, with the house gone and Jack moving into a facility, it felt like the end of an era. Jack tried to put on a brave face, but Emily could see the sadness in his eyes.

"I never thought it would come to this," he said quietly as they settled into his new room, "but I know it's the only way."

Emily choked back tears, feeling a mix of guilt, relief, and grief. She hated that her father had to give up so much to get the care he needed, but she was also grateful that Medicaid would now cover his nursing home stay. At least Jack would be safe, cared for, and not alone. She reminded herself that this was the best decision for him, even if it was hard to accept.

Finding Compassion in the System

As the weeks passed, Emily realized that, while the process had been painful, the nursing home was the right place for Jack. The staff were kind, and Jack was making new friends. He had access to physical therapy, medical care, and activities that kept him engaged. Emily could visit without the constant stress of managing his care on her own. She could just be his daughter again, and that brought her a sense of peace.

Still, the emotional toll of the process—the spend-down, the transition from Medicare to Medicaid, and the sale of the family home—was a stark reminder of the realities of aging in America. It felt unfair that, after a lifetime of hard work, Jack had to lose nearly everything to afford the care he needed in his final years. Emily often thought about other families going through the same experience, wondering how many were grappling with the same feelings of loss and helplessness.

Planning for the Future

Emily wished she had known more about Medicaid earlier. If she could go back, she would have consulted an elder care attorney sooner and planned for Jack's long-term care. She realized that, while the system is flawed, there are resources to help families navigate it. She hoped other families could learn from her experience—by understanding Medicare and Medicaid, planning for the spend-down process, and seeking professional advice before a crisis hits.

As difficult as the journey had been, Emily found comfort in knowing her father was safe, cared for, and no longer burdened by the financial strain of paying for his care. Jack's dignity and well-being were protected, even if the cost had been heartbreaking.

Conclusion
A System Both Flawed and Essential

Emily's story is one many families can relate to. The transition from Medicare to Medicaid is often filled with emotional and financial struggles, forcing families to confront difficult truths about aging. For many, it feels unfair that their loved ones must lose everything they've worked for to receive the care they need. But at the same time, Medicaid is a lifeline, ensuring that seniors receive the skilled nursing care and support they need when their resources run out.

For caregivers, understanding this process—no matter how painful—is essential. By educating yourself early, seeking legal advice, and preparing for the financial realities of long-term care, you can help ensure that your loved one's final years are spent with dignity, comfort, and care. While the journey may be difficult, you are not alone, and help is available to guide you through it.

A Father's Perspective

I never thought it would come to this. You spend your whole life working, saving, trying to build something for your family, and then, in the blink of an eye, it all starts slipping away. I've always prided myself on being independent. I didn't want to be a burden, didn't want to rely on anyone for my care. But here I am—dependent on my daughter, dependent on a system that's as confusing as it is necessary. It's tough to process.

When I first signed up for Medicare, I thought I was set. After all, it's supposed to be there for people like me, isn't it? I've worked hard, paid my taxes, and put my trust in the system. For a while, it seemed to work just fine—doctor visits, hospital stays, the occasional medication—I never had to worry much. But as my health started to decline, it became clear that Medicare wasn't going to cover the kind of care I really needed.

The first time Emily brought it up—about me needing more help at home—I brushed it off. "I'm fine," I'd say, not wanting her to worry. But deep down, I knew it wasn't true. There were days I struggled to get out of bed, let alone take care of myself. But the idea of having a home health aide, or worse, going to a nursing home? It felt like admitting defeat. I wanted to stay in my home, the place I'd built with my wife, the place where I'd raised my family. How could I leave that behind?

But reality has a way of forcing your hand. When I had my fall and ended up in the hospital, I could see the worry in Emily's eyes. She was scared—scared for me and probably scared of what the future looked like. I knew she was already juggling so much: her job, her family, and now me. And I hated that. I hated being the cause of her stress.

Then we started talking about the costs. Medicare, it turns out, wouldn't cover the kind of long-term care I needed. Sure, they helped with the hospital bills and the short-term therapy afterward, but beyond that? We were on our own. I could see Emily doing the math in her head—how long my savings would last, what it would cost to bring in more help at home, and eventually, the possibility of a nursing home. It was a conversation I never wanted to have. But there we were.

The worst part was realizing that everything I had worked for—all those years of saving, being careful with my money—was going to be drained just so I could get the care I needed. I remember sitting with Emily as we went over the finances, and the numbers just didn't add up. We would have to spend everything before Medicaid could step in. Everything. My savings, my investments, even my home.

I'll never forget the day we made the decision to sell the house. That was a tough day. I'd lived in that home for decades. Every room had a memory: Christmas mornings, Sunday dinners, quiet evenings with my wife. And now, it would be gone. The thought of selling it felt like I was losing more than just a house—it was like I was losing a part of myself, too. But I knew it was the only way. Medicaid would cover my care once my assets were spent down, but until then, it was up to us.

I could see the pain in Emily's eyes, too. She didn't want this any more than I did. She was torn between being my daughter and being my caregiver, trying to balance love with practicality. I hated putting her in that position. But when you reach this stage of life, the decisions aren't easy, and they're rarely fair. Watching everything you've worked for slip away, not because of poor planning or mistakes, but because that's how the system works, is paralyzing.

But as much as it hurt to let go of the house and spend down my savings, there was some relief in knowing that I wouldn't be left without care. Once Medicaid kicked in, I'd be taken care of. I wouldn't be left alone to fend for myself. That brought a strange sense of peace, even though it came at a cost.

I've had a lot of time to think about it, lying here in this nursing home. It's not where I imagined I'd end up, but the staff here are kind, and I'm not struggling on my own anymore. Emily can visit without worrying about every detail of my care. We can just talk, like we used to, without the weight of all those decisions hanging over us.

But the truth is, there's still a part of me that feels robbed. Not just of my home or my savings, but of the future I thought I'd have. I never imagined that my final years would be spent in a place like this, relying on Medicaid to make sure I'm cared for. And while I'm grateful for the help, I can't help but feel that something's wrong with a system that forces you to lose everything before it steps in.

Still, I'm trying to focus on what matters. I'm safe. I'm cared for. And my daughter can go back to being my daughter instead of my caretaker. That's worth something, isn't it?

Additional Resources for Navigating Medicare/Medicaid:

1. **Medicare Rights Center**
   The Medicare Rights Center is a nonprofit organization that helps individuals navigate the Medicare system. They offer free counseling, educational resources, and access to advocates who can answer specific Medicare-related questions, such as coverage limits, eligibility, and appeals.
   - » **Website:** medicarerights.org
   - » **Phone:** 1-800-333-4114

2. **SHIP (State Health Insurance Assistance Program)**
   SHIP provides free, local counseling and assistance to Medicare beneficiaries. SHIP counselors can explain Medicare benefits, assist with billing issues, and help individuals choose the right Medicare plan based on their unique healthcare needs.
   - » **Website:** shiphelp.org

3. **Benefits.gov - Medicaid Eligibility**
   Benefits.gov provides an easy-to-use eligibility tool to help families determine whether their loved one qualifies for Medicaid. It also provides detailed information on each state's Medicaid eligibility rules, asset limits, and the spend-down process.
   - » **Website:** benefits.gov/benefit/606

4. **National Council on Aging (NCOA) - Medicaid Long-Term Services and Supports**
   NCOA offers resources and information on Medicaid's Long-Term Services and Supports (LTSS), which include nursing home care, home health services, and personal care aides. These services are essential for those transitioning from Medicare to Medicaid.
   - » **Website:** ncoa.org

5. **Eldercare Resource Planning**

Eldercare Resource Planning provides expert guidance on Medicaid spend-down strategies, asset protection, and how to navigate the transition from Medicare to Medicaid. They offer personalized consultations and financial planning tools to help families manage long-term care expenses.
   » **Website:** eldercareresourceplanning.org

6. **Center for Medicare Advocacy**
   This nonprofit law organization provides education and legal advocacy to help individuals and families navigate Medicare, especially regarding coverage denials, long-term care, and transitioning to Medicaid. The center also offers free webinars and toolkits for caregivers.
   » **Website:** medicareadvocacy.org

7. **National Academy of Elder Law Attorneys (NAELA)**
   NAELA connects families with elder law attorneys who specialize in Medicaid planning, estate planning, and the legal aspects of long-term care. Elder law attorneys can help protect assets during the Medicaid spend-down process and ensure compliance with state-specific rules.
   » **Website:** naela.org

8. **MyMedicare.gov**
   MyMedicare.gov is the official portal for Medicare beneficiaries, allowing users to view their coverage, track claims, and access personalized information about their benefits. It's an essential tool for caregivers managing a loved one's Medicare plan.
   » **Website:** mymedicare.gov

Chapter 8

The Puzzle of Medications and Doctors

When Sara's phone buzzed in the middle of the night, her heart sank. Another hospital visit for her mother, Mary, who had become a frequent flyer in the emergency room over the past few years. Each time, it was the same story: confusion about her medications, conflicting instructions from different doctors, and another round of tests that only added to the complexity of her care. Sara felt like she was drowning in a sea of medical information, prescriptions, and appointments with specialists she could barely keep track of.

By the time her husband, Mark, arrived at the hospital, Sara was exhausted—emotionally and physically. "How are we supposed to manage all of this?" she asked, her voice heavy with frustration.

Mark squeezed her hand. "We'll figure it out. We must."

It was at that moment that Sara realized just how tangled their lives had become, trying to navigate her mother's care. There were specialists for everything—a cardiologist for her heart, an endocrinologist for her diabetes, a neurologist for her memory issues, and a primary care doctor somewhere in the mix. On top of that, Mary was on more than ten different medications, each with its own set of instructions, side effects, and costs. The sheer magnitude of managing it all was overwhelming. Sara knew they couldn't afford to make mistakes, but the complexity of the situation was paralyzing.

Unfortunately, this story isn't unique. Millions of caregivers face the same challenge of piecing together the puzzle of medications and medical care for their aging parents. Our healthcare system has become so fragmented, with specialists for every condition, but little coordination among them. For caregivers, trying to make sense of it all feels like navigating a maze with no map. Yet, this is one of the most critical aspects of ensuring the well-being of your loved one.

Managing Prescriptions and Understanding Medical Recommendations

One of the biggest challenges caregivers face is managing prescriptions. As your parent ages, they'll likely be prescribed medications for various conditions. It's not uncommon for seniors to take ten or more medications daily. The complexity of keeping track of what each medication does, when it needs to be taken, and how it interacts with others can be daunting. But the stakes are high—proper medication management is often the difference between stability and another hospital visit.

Tips for Managing Medications:

- **Create a Reference List of Medications:**
  Start by making a comprehensive list of all your parent's medications, including the dosage, the time of day they need to be taken, and what each medication is for. This will help ensure nothing is missed and will serve as a quick reference during doctor visits.

- **Use a Pill Organizer:**
  Pill organizers can be lifesavers for caregivers. A weekly or monthly pill organizer ensures that the right pills are taken at the right time. If your parent is taking medications multiple times a day, get one with compartments for morning, afternoon, and evening doses.

- **Set Reminders:**
  Use phone alarms or apps that remind you or your parent when it's time to take their medication. Some apps also allow you to track

whether the medication has been taken, which can provide peace of mind.

- **Review Medications Regularly**:
  Medications should be reviewed at every doctor's appointment, especially when a new prescription is added. Ask the doctor to explain what each medication does, why it's necessary, and how it interacts with other drugs. Don't be afraid to question whether all medications are still needed or if the doses can be adjusted.

- **Talk to a Pharmacist:**
  Pharmacists are an often-overlooked resource. If you're confused about side effects or how medications might interact, consult your pharmacist. They can review your parent's medication list and help flag any potential issues.

The cost of medications can also be a significant burden for caregivers and their loved ones. If the price of prescriptions is a concern, ask the doctor or pharmacist about generic alternatives or prescription assistance programs that can help reduce costs. Staying vigilant about both the financial and medical implications of your parent's prescriptions is crucial.

Coordinating Care Across Different Doctors and Specialists

As Sara and Mark learned with Mary, one of the hardest parts of caregiving is trying to coordinate care across multiple doctors and specialists. Each doctor seems to focus on their specialty without fully considering the bigger picture of your parent's overall health. It's easy to get lost in a sea of appointments, conflicting advice, and incomplete communication between healthcare providers.

Where to Start:

- **Choose a Primary Point of Contact:**
  While your parent may have many specialists, it's important to identify a primary care physician (PCP) who can serve as the central point of contact. The PCP should have a complete view of your parent's medical history and help coordinate care between specialists. If your parent's PCP is not actively managing their overall care, consider finding a geriatrician who specializes in the complex needs of seniors.

- **Request Copies of Medical Records:**
  Every time your parent visits a specialist, request a copy of their medical records or a summary of the visit. Keep these organized in a folder or digital file so you have a complete record of their care history. This will help you track any changes in medications or treatments.

- **Coordinate Appointments:**
  Try to schedule appointments with different specialists close together, so your parent doesn't have to make multiple trips to the doctor. Some caregivers find success in asking for care team meetings where all the specialists can be in one online or physical room to discuss their loved one's care.

- **Communicate Between Doctors:**
  Don't assume that doctors are communicating with each other. Be the bridge between them. After each specialist appointment, send the report or summary to the PCP. You may need to advocate for the coordination of care, especially if doctors have differing opinions about treatment.

- **Use a Care Coordinator:**
  If navigating the healthcare system becomes too overwhelming, consider hiring a care coordinator or geriatric care manager. These

professionals specialize in managing the complexities of healthcare for seniors and can ensure that all the moving parts of your parent's care are working together.

Advocating for Your Parent in a Complex Healthcare System

The healthcare system can be difficult to navigate, but when you're caring for an aging parent, the stakes are even higher. Advocating for your parent becomes critical, as your voice might be the only one ensuring they get the care they deserve. Sara and Mark learned this firsthand when Mary's care started to spiral out of control.

After several hospital stays and lengthy rehab facilities, Mark decided to take control. He learned that Mary could receive physical therapy (PT) and occupational therapy (OT) in her independent living community—a service that had never been mentioned during her previous hospital stays.

Mark became a relentless advocate for his mother, ensuring that she received the services she needed. His persistence cut down Mary's hospital stays and reduced her dependence on rehab facilities. Instead of enduring long hospital stays that left her weak and reliant on a walker, Mary could regain strength at home with PT and OT sessions, transforming her quality of life.

Steps to Advocate for Your Parent:

- **Be Persistent:**
  Don't hesitate to ask questions or challenge decisions made by the healthcare team. If something doesn't feel right, speak up.

- **Know Your Parent's Rights:**
  Learn what services your parent is entitled to under Medicare or

their insurance plan. Home health care, PT, OT, and even in-home nursing care might be available, but often, you must ask for them.

- **Communicate with Doctors:**
  Build relationships with your parent's doctors. Make sure they know your parent's preferences and goals. If your parent wants to avoid being placed in a rehab facility, make that clear and request home health services instead.

- **Follow Up:**
  After every hospital stay or major medical appointment, follow up to ensure that recommendations are implemented. Sometimes, referrals for services like PT or home health can slip through the cracks.

Conclusion
Piecing the Puzzle Together

Managing your parent's medications and medical care is one of the most overwhelming parts of caregiving. It can feel like solving a puzzle with too many pieces, especially when you're coordinating care across multiple doctors and navigating a system that doesn't always make it easy. But by organizing medications, maintaining open lines of communication between healthcare providers, and advocating for your parent's needs, you can ensure they receive the best possible care.

Sara and Mark's story shows the power of persistence and advocacy. By learning to navigate the healthcare system and standing firm in the face of challenges, they transformed Mary's care—and her quality of life. Caregiving is hard, but when you take control of the puzzle, piece by piece, you can help your parent live with dignity, strength, and the support they need.

A Parent's Perspective

I used to think I could manage just fine. I mean, I've always been the one who took care of things—paid the bills, handled the house, and kept track of everything. But now? Now, I feel like I'm just a passenger, swept along by this whirlwind of doctors, medications, and appointments that I can barely keep straight.

When Sara comes by to take me to yet another appointment, I can see the worry in her eyes. She tries not to show it, but I know. I know it's a lot for her. Sometimes, I feel like I'm just a burden, with all these pills and specialists and hospital trips. It's hard to keep track of what all these medications are for—one for my heart, one for my diabetes, something else for the pain in my legs. They're always adding something new. I take them because they tell me to, but truthfully, I can't remember half the names, and I'm not always sure what they do.

Sara's been trying so hard to stay on top of everything. She makes lists, sets reminders on her phone, and uses one of those pill organizers to make sure I take the right pills at the right time. I don't know how she does it. She's got her own life, her own family to look after, but here she is, handling my mess. I'm grateful—God, am I grateful—but it doesn't stop me from feeling guilty about all the trouble I'm causing.

The doctors don't make it easy either. One says one thing, and another says something completely different. I've got a cardiologist for my heart, an endocrinologist for my diabetes, and a neurologist for my memory. Half the time, I'm not even sure if they're talking to each other. They send me home with all these instructions, and it's so overwhelming. I try to follow them, but sometimes it feels like too much. I can't even keep track of which appointment is coming up next or what the latest doctor wants me to do.

The worst part is the hospital trips. Every time Sara gets a call in the middle of the night, I see the panic in her face when she rushes in, and I hate it. I hate putting her through that. It seems like every time I end up there, it's because something got mixed up—too much medication, not enough, or something I shouldn't have taken at all. The doctors fix me up, but when I get back home,

I feel like we're right back where we started, just waiting for the next trip to the ER.

I know Sara's doing her best, and I try to help her by remembering things, by taking my meds when I'm supposed to, but it's hard. My mind isn't what it used to be. She's taken on so much, and I can see it wearing on her. She tries to hide it, but I can tell. And every time she drives me to yet another specialist, I can't help but wonder, "Is this really the way it's supposed to be?"

I miss the days when I could handle things on my own. Now, it feels like my life is one big tangle of doctor's appointments and prescriptions. I never thought I'd be in this position, relying on my daughter to manage my care. But here we are, and I'm doing my best to keep up. I just wish it wasn't so complicated—for both of us.

The truth is, I'm scared sometimes. I don't want to end up in the hospital again. I don't want Sara to feel like she has to drop everything to take care of me. But I don't know how to make it easier for her. I know she'll keep fighting for me, talking to the doctors, making sure I get the care I need, but it feels like too much—too many pills, too many appointments, too much uncertainty.

I just wish we had some answers, some way to make it all make sense. Until then, I guess we just keep going, one appointment, one pill at a time. I hope she knows how much I appreciate everything she's doing. I may not say it enough, but I see it. And I love her for it.

Resources for Managing Medications and Coordinating Care:

1. **MediSafe**
   A user-friendly medication management app that sends alerts to take medications and allows caregivers to monitor adherence.
   - » **Website:** medisafeapp.com

2. **CareZone**
   Tracks medications, refills, and doctor's appointments, and lets caregivers create a list of important health information for easy sharing with healthcare providers.
   - » **Website:** carezone.com

3. **Institute for Safe Medication Practices (ISMP)**
   ISMP is a nonprofit organization focused on preventing medication errors. They provide educational tools and resources for patients and caregivers to safely manage medications.
   - » **Website**: ismp.org

4. **American Geriatrics Society (AGS) - Beers Criteria**
   The AGS Beers Criteria is a list of potentially inappropriate medications for older adults, helping caregivers review their parent's medications and discuss with doctors any needed adjustments.
   - » **Website:** geriatricscareonline.org

5. **RxAssist - Patient Assistance Programs for Medications**
   A comprehensive database of patient assistance programs for medications, listing pharmaceutical companies that offer free or low-cost drugs to people who cannot afford their medications.
   - » **Website:** rxassist.org

6. **Geriatrics Care Online - Medication Management Tools**
   Provides access to tools and guidelines for managing medications in older adults, including advice on managing polypharmacy and preventing adverse drug interactions.
   » **Website:** geriatricscareonline.org

7. **National Council on Patient Information and Education (NCPIE)**
   Focuses on improving communication between patients, caregivers, and healthcare professionals about medication use.
   » **Website:** bemedwise.org

8. **FamilyWize - Prescription Discount Programs**
   Partners with pharmacies to offer a free prescription savings card, helping caregivers save money on prescriptions not fully covered by insurance.
   » **Website:** familywize.org

9. **National Institute on Aging (NIA) - Managing Medications**
   Provides resources for older adults and caregivers on managing multiple medications, understanding side effects, and avoiding medication conflicts.
   » **Website:** nia.nih.gov/health/managing-medications

10. **The National Transitions of Care Coalition (NTOCC)**
    Focuses on improving care transitions for patients, offering resources to help caregivers coordinate with healthcare teams and ensure proper communication between doctors.
    » **Website:** ntocc.org

11. **NeedyMeds - Prescription Savings and Medical Assistance Programs**
    Provides information about programs that help people afford medications and healthcare costs, including free or discounted medications, copay assistance, and local medical services.
    » **Website:** needymeds.org

Summary

Managing medications and coordinating care among multiple doctors can be overwhelming. This chapter offers practical strategies to stay organized, avoid errors, and communicate effectively with healthcare providers. With the right approach, you can ensure your parent receives safe, consistent, and effective care.

Chapter 9

In-Home Care
Can They Stay at Home?

When Emily first realized her father, Jim, couldn't live safely on his own anymore, her heart broke. He had always been fiercely independent, priding himself on managing the house and running errands. But after a fall in the kitchen that left him on the floor for hours, Emily knew something had to change. The thought of moving him into a nursing home terrified her. Jim had spent his whole life in that house, and the idea of uprooting him felt like a betrayal. But as his health continued to decline, Emily was left wondering, *Can he really stay at home?*

This is the question that haunts many caregivers. When a loved one begins to struggle with daily tasks—like walking, dressing, or even remembering to take medications—the future can feel overwhelming. The thought of making these difficult decisions while juggling work, family, and other commitments adds to the weight. For caregivers, the idea of helping their loved one remain at home feels right, but they often don't know where to start.

In-home care is an option that allows seniors to stay in the comfort of their own homes while receiving the help they need. But how do you know when it's time to bring in professional help, what kind of safety modifications are needed, and how services like adult day care can make this transition easier for everyone involved?

Home Care Options: When and How to Hire Professional Help

The idea of hiring in-home care for a loved one can feel intimidating. You may wonder, is it necessary yet? How do I even begin? The truth is caregivers often wait until they're overwhelmed or burned out before seeking professional help. But bringing in support early can reduce stress and prevent accidents, giving both you and your loved one peace of mind.

When to Consider In-Home Care:

There are several signs that it may be time to consider hiring professional in-home care:

- **Difficulty with Daily Tasks:**
  If your loved one is having trouble with basic activities—like bathing, dressing, preparing meals, or managing medications—it's time to think about getting help. These tasks can seem small, but as they become harder for your loved one, their risk of injury or neglect increases.

- **Frequent Falls or Injuries:**
  If your parent has had one or more falls, it's a major red flag. Falls are a leading cause of injury among seniors and can lead to serious complications. Professional caregivers can assist with mobility and reduce the risk of falls by helping with tasks that might otherwise be dangerous.

- **Worsening Health Conditions:**
  If your loved one's health is declining due to chronic conditions (like heart disease, diabetes, or dementia), they may need more frequent monitoring and assistance with their daily routine.

- **Caregiver Burnout:**
  If you find yourself exhausted, stressed, and struggling to balance caregiving with your own life, it's okay to ask for help. Bringing in professional caregivers can provide much-needed relief, allowing you to focus on being a loving son or daughter rather than being overwhelmed by caregiving responsibilities.

Types of In-Home Care

When it's time to hire help, you have options depending on your loved one's needs. Here's a breakdown of common in-home care services:

- **Personal Care Aides:**
  They assist with non-medical tasks like bathing, dressing, cooking, and light housekeeping. Personal care aides are a great option if your loved one needs help with daily activities but doesn't require medical care.

- **Home Health Aides:**
  These professionals provide both personal care and basic medical services, like checking vital signs, managing medications, or helping with mobility devices. Home health aides are usually hired when a loved one has medical needs in addition to requiring assistance with daily tasks.

- **Skilled Nursing Care:**
  If your parent has complex medical needs, skilled nursing care might be necessary. A licensed nurse can provide in-home medical treatments, such as wound care, injections, or physical therapy.

To find a caregiver, start by talking to your parent's doctor or a geriatric care manager for recommendations. Agencies that specialize in home care can also help you find trained professionals who are screened, insured, and match your loved one's needs. It's important to interview potential caregivers to ensure they're a good fit, both in terms of experience and personality.

Safety Modifications: Adapting the Home for Aging Parents

Once you've decided to keep your loved one at home, the next step is making sure their living environment is safe and accessible. This is where many caregivers feel overwhelmed—how do you modify a home for someone who is aging or has physical limitations?

Common Home Safety Modifications

Adapting the home doesn't have to mean a complete renovation. There are small, impactful changes you can make that will increase your parent's safety and comfort. Here are some common modifications:

- **Install Grab Bars and Handrails:**
  Installing grab bars in the bathroom—next to the toilet and in the shower—can prevent falls. Handrails along hallways or staircases provide additional support.

- **Reduce Tripping Hazards:**
  Remove rugs, clutter, or furniture that could cause your loved one to trip. Non-slip mats in the bathroom and kitchen are also crucial, as these are high-risk areas for falls.

- **Improve Lighting:**
  Ensure the home is well-lit, especially in hallways, staircases, and entryways. Motion-sensor lights can help your loved one navigate the house at night without fumbling for switches.

- **Adjust Heights:**
  Make sure that commonly used items—like dishes, clothes, or

medications—are stored at heights your parent can easily reach. Consider adding raised toilet seats and shower chairs to make daily routines safer and more comfortable.

- **Medical Alert Systems:**
  If your loved one is prone to falls or medical emergencies, a medical alert system can be a lifesaver. These devices allow them to call for help with the press of a button.

These modifications might seem minor, but they can have a life-changing impact. For example, when Emily installed grab bars in Jim's bathroom and removed the rugs from his house, Jim's confidence improved. He felt more comfortable living at home, knowing he could move safely around the house.

Adult Day Care Services: A Hidden Gem for Respite and Socialization

One option that often goes unnoticed but can be incredibly helpful is adult day care services. These centers offer daytime care for seniors, providing both social activities and medical supervision in a structured environment. For caregivers, adult day care can be a lifeline, offering a much-needed break while knowing that your parent is safe and engaged.

What Adult Day Care Services Offer

Adult day care services offer a wide range of benefits for both seniors and their caregivers:

- **Socialization:**
  Many seniors who remain at home suffer from loneliness and isolation. Adult day care provides a space for them to socialize with peers, participate in activities, and feel part of a community. Regular socialization is linked to better mental health and reduced

cognitive decline.

- **Medical Supervision:**
  Many centers offer basic medical care, such as medication management, monitoring of chronic conditions, and assistance with personal care needs. This is especially helpful for seniors with conditions like dementia or Parkinson's, who need extra support throughout the day.

- **Respite for Caregivers:**
  For caregivers, the ability to have a few hours or a day to themselves is invaluable. Whether it's to go to work, run errands, or simply rest, adult day care allows you to step away from caregiving knowing your loved one is in good hands.

Finding Adult Day Care Services

To find adult day care services, start by looking for programs in your area through your local **Area Agency on Aging**. These centers are often affordable—some are even Medicaid-covered or offer sliding scale fees based on income. You can also visit the centers with your parent to get a feel for the environment and make sure it's a place where they'll be comfortable and engaged.

Conclusion
The Path to Independence at Home

The question of whether your loved one can stay at home is difficult, and it's one many caregivers wrestle with. But with the right support, safety modifications, and community resources, it's possible for seniors to age in place and maintain their independence in the home they love.

For Emily and her father, Jim, a combination of in-home care and safety modifications made all the difference. Jim was able to stay in the house he cherished, with a sense of security and comfort. And Emily found peace knowing she had taken the right steps to ensure her father's well-being.

If you're on this journey, remember—you're not alone. There are options, resources, and people ready to help. Take one step at a time, and you can create a plan that works for both you and your loved one.

A Father's Perspective

I never thought I'd end up here, wondering if I can still live in my own home. For so many years, I've prided myself on handling everything—taking care of the house, running errands, keeping things in order. It wasn't even a question. But now? Now, after that fall in the kitchen, I can't help but feel like everything's slipping out of my hands. I've always been strong and capable, but lately, it's getting harder to manage the simplest things.

Emily keeps bringing it up—gently, of course. She's worried. I see it in her eyes every time she visits. After that fall, she started talking about in-home care, as if I can't manage things on my own anymore. And part of me feels like I'm losing the battle. I know she means well, but this is my home. I've lived here for decades, raised my family here.

The thought of leaving or needing someone else to help me live in my own space ... it feels like a betrayal of everything I've worked so hard to maintain.

I don't want to be a burden. I don't want Emily running herself ragged worrying about me, but I also don't want to give up this life I've built. This is my home. These walls hold memories—of my wife, my kids, grandkids, and all the years that have passed. How can I just let that go? Even the idea of having someone come in to help me feels like admitting defeat. But deep down, I know things aren't the same. My legs aren't as steady, my balance is off, and I don't trust myself as much anymore. The fall scared me, more than I'd like to admit.

Emily talks about hiring someone to help with the little things—like cooking, bathing, or just making sure I don't trip over the rugs. She even mentioned something about grab bars and reorganizing the house to make things safer for me. It's hard to wrap my head around the idea of needing someone to assist with things I've done my whole life. It makes me feel ... old. And I hate that. I've always been independent. Always been able to take care of myself. But I can't deny that getting around the house isn't as easy as it used to be.

The truth is, the idea of moving into a facility terrifies me. The thought of leaving this place ... it feels like I'd be giving up everything that makes me, well, me. I know Emily is just trying to keep me safe. I know she's juggling her job, her family, and me on top of it all. And I can see that it's wearing her down. The last thing I want is for her to feel like she has to take on everything by herself.

Maybe she's right. Maybe it's time to think about in-home care, even if it's just a little help here and there. It doesn't mean I've lost my independence, right? If it lets me stay in my own home, then maybe it's worth considering. I want to feel safe here again, and I don't want to keep worrying Emily.

CRACK THE CODE

And if making a few changes to the house—like getting rid of those damned rugs and putting in some grab bars—helps keep me from falling again, then maybe it's a good idea. The truth is, I want to stay here, where I belong. But I also don't want to be a burden. Emily doesn't deserve that.

It's hard to accept that I can't do everything on my own anymore. But if in-home care means I can keep living here, with a bit of dignity and peace of mind, then maybe I need to swallow my pride. I just hope that by making these changes, I can hold onto this place—and myself—a little longer. Maybe, just maybe, it's the right thing to do. For both of us.

Helpful Resources

1. **National Institute on Aging (NIA) – Home Care Services**
   The NIA provides comprehensive information on how to assess in-home care needs, find caregivers, and modify homes for safety.
   » **Website:** https://www.nia.nih.gov/health/caregiving/services-older-adults-living-home

2. **National Association for Home Care & Hospice (NAHC)**
   NAHC offers a directory of certified home care agencies and provides guides on understanding home health care, payment options, and safety.
   » **Website**: nahc.org

3. **Eldercare Locator – Adult Day Care Services Finder**
   Eldercare Locator connects seniors and caregivers with local adult day care services, in-home care providers, and respite services.
   » **Website:** eldercare.acl.gov

4. **AgingCare.com – Comprehensive Caregiver Resources**
   AgingCare.com offers articles, discussion forums, and expert

advice on in-home care, managing caregiving tasks, and ensuring your loved one's safety at home.
   » **Website:** agingcare.com

5. **Family Caregiver Alliance – Caregiving for Your Elderly Parent**
   FCA provides resources for family caregivers, including tips on managing stress, balancing caregiving, and preventing burnout.
   » **Website:** caregiver.org

6. **National Council on Aging (NCOA) – Fall Prevention Resources**
   NCOA offers guides on making homes safer for aging parents, including how to assess fall risks and implement necessary home modifications.
   » **Website:** https://www.ncoa.org/professionals/health/prevention/falls-prevention/

7. **Program of All-Inclusive Care for the Elderly (PACE)**
   PACE is a Medicare and Medicaid program that provides all-inclusive care, often allowing seniors to remain at home while receiving comprehensive medical and social services.
   » **Website:** pace4you.org
   »

8. **Medicare.gov – Home Health Services**
   Medicare.gov provides comprehensive details on what home health services Medicare covers and how to qualify for them.
   » **Website:** https://www.medicare.gov/coverage/home-health-services

Chapter 10

When Assisted Living is the Next Step

Marjorie had always been an independent woman, but as she approached her late 80s, the house that had once been her pride and joy started to feel more like a burden. Her garden, which she used to tend daily, had become overgrown, and the stairs to her bedroom felt steeper with each passing day. She was lonely, spending her time in the same worn chair by the window, watching the world outside but no longer feeling like she was a part of it. Her daughter, Jane, noticed the change every time she visited. Marjorie seemed more withdrawn, quieter, and had stopped cooking the meals she used to love.

The conversation about assisted living had come up a few times, but each time, Marjorie resisted. She didn't want to leave her home and didn't want to lose her independence. "I'm fine here," she'd say, even though Jane knew better. It wasn't until Marjorie had a fall and spent several days in the hospital that Jane realized they had no choice but to make a change.

At first, the decision to move Marjorie into an assisted living community felt overwhelming. Jane wondered if she was doing the right thing—if she was betraying her mother's wishes. But she also knew her mother needed help, and she couldn't provide the care Marjorie needed while balancing her own job and family.

The first few months were hard for both. Marjorie missed her home, the familiar smells, and the memories tied to every corner. Jane worried constantly—had she made the right decision? But slowly, things began to change. Marjorie started making friends in the community, joining activities, and rediscovering her love of cooking in the communal kitchen. The isolation that had weighed her down for years began to lift. She was laughing again, finding joy in her new routine, and Jane saw her mother coming back to life.

How to Know When It's Time for Assisted Living

One of the hardest decisions a caregiver will face is knowing when it's time for assisted living. The signs can be subtle at first, but they often build up over time. You might notice your parent is becoming more forgetful, less engaged with life, or physically unable to maintain their home. They may start having difficulty with daily tasks, like cooking, cleaning, or even dressing. For many caregivers, the decision is triggered by a fall or medical emergency that forces them to confront the reality that their loved one can no longer live safely at home.

Here are some signs that it might be time to consider assisted living:

- **Difficulty Managing Daily Activities:**
  If your parent is struggling to manage daily tasks—like preparing meals, maintaining personal hygiene, or managing their medications—it may be time to explore assisted living options.

- **Frequent Falls or Health Declines:**
  Physical limitations or chronic health issues can make living at home dangerous. If your loved one has had multiple falls or is experiencing frequent hospital stays, assisted living might provide a safer environment.

- **Social Isolation:**
  Loneliness can have a significant impact on a senior's mental and physical health. If your parent is becoming increasingly isolated, an assisted living community can offer much-needed social interaction and support.

- **Memory Problems:**
  If your parent is experiencing memory loss or dementia, they may need the specialized care that memory care communities provide. These communities are designed to support those with cognitive decline, offering a structured environment and trained staff who understand the unique challenges of dementia. This topic is covered in more detail in the next chapter.

What to Look for in an Assisted Living Community: Red Flags and Green Lights

Once you've decided that assisted living is the next step, the process of finding the right community can feel daunting. There are several factors to consider—location, amenities, the quality of care, and the overall atmosphere. But knowing what to look for and what to avoid can make the decision easier.

Green Lights: Signs of a Great Community

- **Engaged and Happy Residents:**
  When you visit a community, take note of how the residents interact with each other and with the staff. Do they seem happy, engaged, and comfortable? A thriving community will have active residents who are participating in activities, socializing, and enjoying their surroundings.

- **Caring and Compassionate Staff:**
  The attitude of the staff is crucial. Look for caregivers who are patient, kind, and attentive. You want to know that your parent will be treated with dignity and respect.

- **Variety of Activities:**
  Assisted living should offer more than just basic care. Look for

a community that provides a range of activities—like exercise classes, art programs, outings, and social events. Staying active and engaged is key to a fulfilling life in assisted living.

- **Clean and Well-Maintained Facilities:**
  A clean, well-kept environment is a good sign that the community is well-managed. Look beyond the common areas—visit the dining room, peek into the resident apartments, and check out the outdoor spaces.

- **Visit After Hours:**
  Show up on the weekend or after regular business hours to get a feel for community life outside of what's presented on a planned tour. Talk with residents and get a sense of their level of happiness and satisfaction.

Red Flags: What to Avoid

- **Unresponsive or Overworked Staff:**
  If the staff seems rushed, overwhelmed, or unresponsive to residents' needs, this is a big warning sign. A high staff-to-resident ratio is crucial for ensuring your loved one gets the attention they need.

- **Unhappy Residents:**
  If the residents seem disengaged, bored, or unhappy, that's a red flag. Assisted living is about providing not just care, but a sense of community and purpose. A lack of social engagement could indicate poor management or limited opportunities for activities.

- **High Staff Turnover:**
  Frequent changes in staff can be a sign of poor management. Consistent staffing is important for building relationships between caregivers and residents and for ensuring continuity of care. Ask specifically how long the Executive Director has been there, as their leadership is critical to a vibrant community life.

- **Neglect of Personal Care:**
  If residents appear unkempt, if rooms are dirty, or if there are signs of neglect, this is a major red flag. Pay close attention to how well residents' personal needs are being met.

The Emotional Transition: For You and Your Parent

Moving into assisted living is a big transition, and it can be emotionally challenging for both you and your parent. The first few months are often the hardest, as your parent adjusts to their new environment and both of you navigate the emotional complexities of this change. It's important to remember that these feelings are normal—and temporary.

For your parent, the fear of losing independence and leaving behind the familiarity of home can be overwhelming. They may experience feelings of grief, resistance, and even guilt for needing help. For you, the emotional toll of seeing your parent struggle with this transition, and the weight of feeling responsible for their well-being, can lead to feelings of doubt and anxiety.

Easing the Transition

- **Visit Regularly:**
  During the first few months, visit as often as you can. This provides reassurance to your parent that they are not alone in this new chapter. It also allows you to monitor how they are adjusting and address any concerns they may have.

- **Encourage Social Engagement:**
  Help your parent get involved in the community's activities. Encourage them to attend social events, join group activities, or even just have lunch with new neighbors. The more engaged they are, the quicker they'll start to feel at home. Be sure to ask

the community to pair your loved one up with a friend who can show them the ropes, as this can have a tremendous impact on their experience.

- **Be Patient:**
It's important to give your parent time to adjust. Moving into a new environment can be unsettling, and it's natural for them to need a few months to fully adapt. Be patient, offer emotional support, and remind them that this is about improving their quality of life, not taking away their independence.

- **Stay Positive:**
Your attitude can have a big impact on how your parent feels about the move. Even if you're feeling uncertain, try to remain positive about the benefits of assisted living. Highlight the social opportunities, the activities, and the peace of mind that comes with knowing they'll have help whenever they need it.

What Does Assisted Living Cost and How to Pay for It?

One of the biggest questions caregivers have when considering assisted living is, how much will this cost, and how can we pay for it? Unfortunately, families are surprised to learn that Medicare does not cover the cost of assisted living. However, there are still ways to manage the financial burden.

Understanding the Costs

According to the National Center for Assisted Living (NCAL), the cost of assisted living varies widely depending on location, services, and the level of care needed. On average, it can range from $3,000 to $7,000 per month (as of 2024).

Ways to Pay for Assisted Living

- **Personal Savings:**
  Families use personal savings, retirement funds, or the sale of a home to pay for assisted living. If your parent has planned for long-term care, this may be the primary source of funding.

- **Long-Term Care Insurance:**
  If your parent has long-term care insurance, it may cover part or all of the cost of assisted living. Review their policy to understand what is covered and the conditions for receiving benefits.

- **Veterans Benefits:**
  If your parent is a veteran, they may qualify for Aid and Attendance benefits through the VA, which can help cover the cost of assisted living.

- **Medicaid:**
  In some cases, Medicaid may help cover the cost of assisted living, but eligibility varies by state and is typically based on income and assets. Medicaid primarily covers skilled nursing care, so you'll need to research what's available in your area for assisted living, as some communities set aside a certain number of apartments for Medicaid residents.

- **Reverse Mortgages or Bridge Loans:**
  Some families choose to use a reverse mortgage or take out a bridge loan to cover the cost of assisted living until other financial resources become available.

- **Life Insurance Policies:**
  A life insurance policy can sometimes be used to help pay for assisted living, but this typically requires converting the policy into a liquid asset or using specific financial options associated with life

insurance. Consult with a financial advisor to understand the best way to use a life insurance policy to cover assisted living expenses.

A Mother's Perspective

I never thought I'd be here, sitting in this new apartment in an assisted living community, trying to make sense of it all. For years, I've been so sure that I'd stay in my own home until the very end. I loved that house—every room filled with memories, every corner a reminder of the life I built with my family. But then, things started to change, and suddenly, the house didn't feel like the same safe haven it once was. The stairs became harder to climb, and the garden I once adored was too much for me to keep up with. I found myself spending more time alone, just staring out the window, feeling more and more disconnected from the world outside.

I know my daughter, Jane, noticed. She's always been so patient, checking in on me, helping where she could. But I could see the worry in her eyes each time she visited. I tried to pretend everything was fine—tried to convince both of us that I could still manage on my own. Even after that fall, I told myself it was just a fluke. I wasn't ready to admit that things were changing, that maybe I couldn't do it all by myself anymore.

The conversation about assisted living had come up a few times, and each time, I pushed back. I wasn't ready to leave my home. I wasn't ready to lose my independence. But after the hospital stay, there was no denying it. I needed more help than Jane could give, and staying at home just wasn't safe anymore. It broke my heart to think about leaving, and I could see it broke Jane's heart, too. She didn't want to force me into something I wasn't ready for, but she knew it was time. We both did.

The first few months here were hard. I missed my home more than I thought possible—the smell of the garden after it rained, the familiar creak of the floorboards, the feeling of being surrounded by all those years of memories. I felt like a stranger in my own life, living in a place that didn't yet feel like home. I know Jane was worried, constantly checking in, making sure I was adjusting. I could see she was second-guessing the decision, wondering if she'd done the right thing by moving me here. And I have to admit, I wondered the same.

But slowly, things started to change. It wasn't immediate, but little by little, I found my footing. I began to get to know some of the other residents—people who were going through the same struggles as I was, trying to find their place in this new chapter of life. The staff were kind, and I started joining some of the activities—bingo, a cooking class, even a book club. I hadn't realized how lonely I'd been until I wasn't anymore.

There was a day not too long ago when I caught myself laughing with a group of friends in the common room, and it hit me—this wasn't the end of my independence; it was just a new kind of freedom. I wasn't stuck in that old chair by the window anymore, watching life go by. I was part of a community again. I was cooking in the communal kitchen, having lunch with new friends, and even planning to join a trip to the botanical gardens. It felt good, better than I'd expected, to be around people again, to have help when I needed it, but still live my own life.

Don't get me wrong—I still miss my home. I don't think that feeling will ever go away entirely. But I also see now that moving here wasn't about losing my independence. It was about gaining the support I needed to keep living fully. I wasn't ready to admit it back then, but Jane was right. I wasn't living anymore—I was just getting by, and that's not the life I want. Now, I'm starting to feel like myself again.

I know Jane still worries, but I can see she's more at peace with the decision, just like I am. She doesn't have to carry the weight of my care alone anymore, and that makes me feel better too. We're both finding a new normal, and in a strange way, this place is becoming part of that.

It's hard to let go, harder than I ever imagined. But I've learned that moving into assisted living isn't about giving up—it's about finding a way to keep living, even when life changes. And maybe that's the most important lesson I've learned through all of this: that letting go doesn't mean losing yourself. It just means making space for something new.

Resources for In-Home Care, Safety Modifications, and Assisted Living

- **Home Care Association of America (HCAOA)**
  HCAOA provides resources for families seeking in-home care services, including a directory of home care providers across the U.S.
  - » **Website:** www.hcaoa.org

- **National Association for Home Care & Hospice (NAHC)**
  NAHC offers resources on home care and hospice services, including a search tool for licensed home care providers.
  - » **Website:** www.nahc.org

- **Rebuilding Together**
  A nonprofit that provides home modifications and repairs for low-income homeowners, particularly seniors.
  - » **Website:** www.rebuildingtogether.org

- **CareLinx**
  An online platform that helps families find in-home caregivers and provides support with caregiving management tools.
  - » **Website:** www.carelinx.com

- **National Adult Day Services Association (NADSA)**
  NADSA offers a directory of adult day care centers nationwide and resources for caregivers.
  - » **Website:** www.nadsa.org

- **Aging in Place - Home Modification Resources**
  Aging in Place provides information on making homes safer for seniors, offering a list of certified home modification contractors.
  - » **Website:** www.aginginplace.org

- **National Institute on Aging (NIA) - Home Safety and Fall Prevention**
  The NIA offers guides on home safety and fall prevention for seniors.
  - » **Website:** https://www.nia.nih.gov/site-search?search=fall+prevention

- **Philips Lifeline - Medical Alert Systems**
  Offers medical alert systems for seniors at risk of falling or needing immediate assistance.
  - » **Website:** https://www.lifeline.com/

- **Meals on Wheels America**
  Provides home-delivered meals to seniors who are unable to prepare food themselves.
  - » **Website:** www.mealsonwheelsamerica.org

Chapter 11

Memory Care and Dementia
The Long Goodbye

When Rebecca's mother, Linda, began forgetting small things—where she put her keys, the names of neighbors she'd known for years—Rebecca brushed it off as normal aging. But when Linda started getting lost in her own neighborhood and forgot how to cook the family's favorite meals, Rebecca couldn't ignore it anymore. After several doctor's visits, tests, and referrals, the diagnosis came: Alzheimer's disease. It was a word that hit like a punch to the gut, even though Rebecca had suspected it for months. This wasn't just normal aging—this was something that would slowly and painfully take her mother away.

For the next two years, Rebecca did her best to care for Linda at home. She helped her mother with meals, reminded her to take medications, and watched helplessly as Linda struggled to recognize familiar faces, including her own grandchildren. It became increasingly difficult, both emotionally and physically. When Linda started wandering at night and having episodes of confusion that led to anger, Rebecca realized she couldn't do it alone anymore. The decision to move Linda to a memory care community was the hardest thing Rebecca had ever done. It felt like giving up, like she was abandoning her mother. But deep down, Rebecca knew it was the right choice—Linda needed the kind of specialized care she simply couldn't provide.

This chapter is for those facing the same painful reality. Dementia and Alzheimer's disease are heartbreaking conditions that slowly steal away the person you love. The term "long goodbye" is often used to describe the gradual decline that occurs with these diseases. While moving a loved one into memory care may feel like surrender, it's often the best decision for both the caregiver and the person with dementia. Understanding the disease, the difference in care needed, and the emotional toll it takes can help families navigate this incredibly difficult journey.

Understanding Dementia, Alzheimer's, and Other Cognitive Declines

Dementia is not a specific disease but a general term used to describe a decline in cognitive ability severe enough to interfere with daily life. It affects memory, thinking, language, and problem-solving. Alzheimer's disease is the most common form of dementia, accounting for 60-80% of cases, but there are other types as well, including vascular dementia, Lewy body dementia, and frontotemporal dementia.

- **Alzheimer's Disease:** A progressive brain disorder that slowly destroys memory and thinking skills. In its advanced stages, individuals lose the ability to conduct even the simplest tasks, such as eating or dressing.

- **Vascular Dementia:** Often caused by a stroke or damage to the blood vessels in the brain. Symptoms can vary but may include difficulties with reasoning, planning, judgment, and memory.

- **Lewy Body Dementia:** Characterized by abnormal protein deposits in the brain, leading to memory loss, confusion, hallucinations, and physical symptoms like Parkinson's disease.

- **Frontotemporal Dementia:** Affects the frontal and temporal lobes of the brain, leading to personality changes, difficulty with language, and impaired decision-making.

These conditions progress at different rates, but all result in severe cognitive decline over time. Unfortunately, there is no cure for dementia, and treatments can only help manage symptoms for a limited period.

How Memory Care Differs from Traditional Assisted Living

Memory care is a specialized form of care designed for individuals with Alzheimer's, dementia, or other cognitive impairments. It goes beyond what is typically offered in traditional assisted living communities, providing an environment specifically tailored to the needs of those experiencing memory loss.

Here's how memory care differs:

- **Specialized Care and Training:**
  Staff in memory care communities are specifically trained to work with individuals with dementia. They understand how to manage confusion, agitation, wandering, and behavioral changes in ways that traditional caregivers may not. They use techniques to redirect and calm residents when they are upset or confused.

- **Safety and Security:**
  Memory care units are designed with safety in mind. They are typically secured to prevent wandering, with alarm systems and locked doors to ensure that residents don't leave the premises unsupervised. The environment is arranged to be familiar and comfortable, helping reduce anxiety and disorientation.

- **Structured Routines:**
  People with dementia often feel more secure with a consistent routine. Memory care communities offer structured days that include meals, activities, and rest periods at the same times each day, which helps reduce anxiety and confusion.

- **Therapeutic Activities:**
  Memory care communities focus on activities that stimulate cognitive function and promote emotional well-being. These might include music therapy, art therapy, pet therapy, and other sensory-based activities designed to connect residents with their surroundings and create moments of joy, even as their cognitive abilities decline.

- **Higher Staff-to-Resident Ratio:**
  Memory care communities typically have a higher staff-to-resident ratio than traditional assisted living. This ensures that residents receive more personalized care and attention, which is crucial when dealing with the complexities of dementia.

The Emotional Toll of Memory Loss on Caregivers

Caring for someone with dementia is one of the most emotionally taxing experiences a person can face. Watching a loved one lose their memories, their ability to communicate, and their sense of self can feel like grieving someone who is still physically present. Caregivers often describe the experience as a "long goodbye," where you slowly lose the person you once knew, bit by bit.

For Rebecca, the hardest part wasn't just the memory loss—it was the personality changes. The mother, who had always been gentle and kind, sometimes became angry, even accusing her of stealing or lying. "That's not my mother," Rebecca would think, heartbroken. But at the same time, it was. That paradox is one of the cruelest aspects of dementia.

The emotional toll on caregivers is immense. You may feel:

- **Grief:** Watching your loved one slip away, even as they are still physically present, leads to feelings of loss and sadness.
- **Guilt:** Moving a loved one into memory care often comes with

feelings of guilt, as though you've failed them by not being able to care for them at home.
- **Exhaustion:** The demands of caregiving are intense, and trying to manage it alone can lead to physical and emotional exhaustion.
- **Frustration and Anger:** It's normal to feel frustrated or angry when your loved one no longer recognizes you, repeats questions, or becomes agitated. These feelings are a natural part of the caregiving journey.

Recognizing the emotional toll and finding ways to cope is critical. Support groups, therapy, and leaning on family and friends can make a world of difference during this challenging time.

How Long Does Someone Live After Entering Memory Care?

One of the most difficult questions families face is how long their loved one will live after being diagnosed with dementia or after moving into memory care. The answer varies depending on the type of dementia, the person's overall health, and how far the disease has progressed.

According to the Alzheimer's Association, individuals with Alzheimer's may live anywhere from 4 to 8 years after diagnosis, though some live as long as 10 to 20 years. Once a person moves into memory care, they are typically in the moderate to advanced stages of the disease, meaning their cognitive decline is significant. While it's impossible to predict an exact timeline, many residents live for 2 to 5 years after entering memory care.

What's most important during this time is to spend quality time with your loved one while you can. As their ability to communicate diminishes, it's the simple things—holding hands, listening to music together, sharing a quiet moment—that matter most. Even in the late stages, your presence can bring them comfort and joy.

How to Pay for Memory Care

Memory care can be expensive, and it's essential to explore all options for covering the cost. Many families use a combination of personal savings, long-term care insurance, veterans' benefits, and Medicaid to pay for memory care services. Some states also offer Medicaid waivers for memory care, but eligibility and coverage vary.

A Story of Hope: Finding Light in the Dark

Rebecca was scared the day she moved Linda into memory care, afraid she was abandoning her mother at a time when she needed her most. The first few months were tough—Linda was confused and angry, and Rebecca questioned her decision every day. But then something shifted. The staff at the memory care community worked patiently with Linda, helping her feel safe and secure. They introduced her to music therapy, and the moment Linda heard her favorite songs from the 1950s, her face lit up. For the first time in months, Rebecca saw a glimpse of her mother's old self.

Over time, Rebecca saw the peace that the memory care setting brought Linda. While the disease continued to take its toll, Linda seemed calmer, more content, and less frightened. The burden that had weighed heavily on Rebecca's shoulders began to lift. She knew she had made the right decision, not only for her mother but for herself. Though the disease was stealing Linda's memories, it couldn't steal the moments of connection they still shared.

Conclusion
The Long Goodbye and Finding Peace

Memory care is often the next step in the heartbreaking journey of dementia. While the decision to move a loved one into such a community is never easy, it can provide them with the specialized care and support they need to live their final years in dignity and comfort.

The emotional toll of memory loss is profound, but it's important to remember that you don't have to face it alone. Memory care communities are designed to provide not only the physical care your loved one needs but also the emotional support that you, as a caregiver, desperately need. Embrace the time you have left with your loved one, knowing that even though they may forget things, they will never forget the love that connects you.

A Mother's Perspective

It's hard to describe how it feels, knowing that piece by piece, I'm losing myself. There are moments when I catch a glimpse of what's happening—when I forget something simple, like a familiar face or the way to the store. I can see the worry in my daughter's eyes, even though she tries to hide it. I try to laugh it off, pretend it's no big deal, but deep down, I know something is slipping away from me.

I used to be so sure of myself—raising my kids, managing the house, being the strong one. But now, everything seems harder. I forget the names of people I've known for years. I wander into a room and have no idea why I'm there. My daughter tells me I've asked her the same question three times, but I don't remember even asking once. And every time it happens, I feel this pit in my stomach, this fear that I'm disappearing from the inside out.

I've always prided myself on being independent, and the thought of losing that is terrifying. I see it in my daughter's face, too—Rebecca. She's always been so patient with me, gently reminding me of things I forget. But I can see the exhaustion in her eyes. She's juggling her family, her work, and now me. I never wanted to be a burden to her, and yet here we are.

When she first brought up memory care, I resisted. How could I leave my home? How could I let go of the life I built, the memories tied to every corner of my house? I told her I could manage—I'd be fine. But then I started forgetting more and more. The fall was the breaking point. I knew then that it wasn't just about me anymore. I could see the fear in Rebecca's face, and I realized I couldn't keep pretending everything was okay.

Moving into memory care wasn't easy. It felt like I was giving up, like I was losing another part of myself. I thought about all the moments I'd miss in my own home—the smell of fresh coffee brewing, the sound of my old clock ticking in the hallway. But I could also see how exhausted Rebecca was, trying to manage it all. I didn't want to make things harder for her.

The first few weeks in memory care were tough. I felt confused, lost, and out of place. I missed my home. I missed my life. But slowly, things began to change. The staff here, they know what I'm going through. They don't get frustrated when I ask the same question again or when I forget what day it is. They're patient, kind, and somehow, they make me feel safe.

One day, they played an old song, something from the 1950s; oh, it was "Johnny B. Goode" by Chuck Berry (How do I know that?) and for the first time in a long while, I felt like myself again. Music has this way of cutting through the fog, of reaching something deep inside me that's still there, even when everything else feels like it's slipping away. And when Rebecca visits, we sit together and listen to those songs, and for a little while, it feels like the old days. I know she's hurting, too—watching me change, watching me fade—but I can tell she's found some peace knowing I'm being cared for.

It's strange, this feeling of knowing you're losing your memories but somehow still holding on to the love you feel. I may forget names, places, or even faces, but the love between my daughter and me—that's something this disease can't take. I see it in her eyes when she visits. I hear it in her voice when she asks how I'm feeling. And even if I can't remember the details, I know she's there, and that brings me comfort.

I never imagined my life would end up like this—living in a place where other people have to remind me of the things I used to know so well. But I'm learning to accept it, to find peace in the little things. The hugs from my daughter, the songs that bring back pieces of my past, the moments of connection that still make me feel alive. Even if I can't remember everything, I know I'm still loved, and that's what matters most.

I may be saying goodbye to parts of myself, but I know Rebecca is holding on to those memories for me. And as long as she's there, I'm not really gone.

Resources for Memory Care, Dementia, and Caregiver Support

1. **MemoryCare**
   A nonprofit organization providing specialized medical care to those living with cognitive impairments such as Alzheimer's disease and other dementias. They offer family consultations, caregiver education, and long-term care planning.
   » **Website:** memorycare.org

2. **Dementia Society of America**
   Provides education and resources for all forms of dementia. They also offer grants to fund dementia care services and respite care for families.
   » **Website:** dementiasociety.org

3. **Alzheimer's Foundation of America (AFA)**
   AFA offers resources such as a toll-free helpline, educational materials, and respite care grants.
   » **Website:** alzfdn.org
   » **Phone:** 1-866-232-8484

4. **Teepa Snow's Positive Approach to Care (PAC)**
   Renowned dementia care expert Teepa Snow provides workshops, videos, and practical tips on caregiving for dementia patients.
   » **Website:** teepasnow.com

5. **The Association for Frontotemporal Degeneration (AFTD)**
   AFTD provides resources and support for families affected by frontotemporal degeneration.
   » **Website:** theaftd.org

6. **Lewy Body Dementia Association (LBDA)**
   The LBDA provides education, resources, and support for those affected by Lewy body dementia.
   » **Website:** lbda.org

7. **The Eden Alternative**
   A global nonprofit dedicated to improving the quality of life for elders and caregivers, focusing on person-centered care for those with cognitive decline.
   » **Website:** edenalt.org

8. **Eldercare Locator – Dementia Care Resources**
   Connects families with local dementia care services, support groups, and memory care options.
   - » **Website:** eldercare.acl.gov
   - » **Phone:** 1-800-677-1116

9. **Family Caregiver Alliance (FCA) – Dementia Caregiving**
   FCA offers educational materials and support specifically for caregivers of individuals with dementia.
   - » **Website:** caregiver.org

10. **Medicare's Guide to Alzheimer's Disease and Related Dementias**
    Provides information on how Medicare can help pay for services related to Alzheimer's and other dementias.
    - » **Website:** https://www.medicare.gov/coverage

Chapter 12

Considering Independent Living—A Step Toward Maintaining Independence with Support

You aren't at the point where your loved one needs assisted living or memory care, but you are noticing changes in health, increased isolation, and a sense that it's time for a change. Independent living might be the perfect option for your mom or dad at this stage of life. For seniors like my own mom, the thought of moving from their home to any kind of senior living community can feel overwhelming, even when they recognize that living alone has become increasingly difficult. Independent living offers a unique middle ground—combining the freedom of living independently with the convenience of supportive services and a built-in community. It's an option that allows seniors to maintain their lifestyle without the daily stress of managing a household.

Why Consider Independent Living?

Independent living is ideal for older adults who are still relatively active but may want to downsize from a larger home or alleviate some of the burdens of maintaining it. It's a great option for those who don't yet need help with daily activities like dressing or bathing but might want assistance with things like housekeeping, transportation, or meal preparation.

Here's why independent living might be the right option for your loved one:

- **Freedom from Home Maintenance:**
  Maintaining a home can become overwhelming as we age. Independent living communities typically offer services like housekeeping, laundry, and home maintenance. This means no more worries about mowing the lawn, shoveling snow, or fixing the leaky faucet.

- **Convenience and Amenities:**
  Independent living communities are designed to make life easier. Many offer on-site dining, transportation to doctor's appointments, and a wide range of amenities, such as fitness centers, swimming pools, libraries, and social clubs. These amenities make it easy for residents to stay active and engaged in a vibrant community.

- **Social Opportunities:**
  Loneliness and isolation can take a toll on seniors living alone. In an independent living community, residents have access to a wide variety of social activities, from exercise classes to group outings and communal meals. This sense of community can significantly improve mental and emotional well-being by helping seniors stay connected to others.

- **Security and Peace of Mind:**
  Many independent living communities provide 24/7 security and on-site staff for emergencies, giving both the resident and their family peace of mind. Knowing that help is always available can alleviate worries about safety, especially for seniors who live alone and might experience falls or other health issues.

- **Flexibility for the Future:**
  Some independent living communities are part of life plan communities (also known as continuing care retirement communities, or CCRCs), which allow residents to transition to higher levels of care—such as assisted living or memory care—as their needs change. This provides flexibility and ensures that

residents won't have to move again if they require more support in the future.

What Does Independent Living Cost?

The cost of independent living can vary widely depending on the location, the size of the apartment, and the types of services offered. On average, independent living communities range from $2,000 to $5,000 per month. This typically includes rent, utilities, and access to amenities, but additional services—such as meals or housekeeping—may come at an extra cost.

Independent living is often paid for through personal savings, retirement funds, or the sale of a home. Unlike nursing homes, Medicare and Medicaid do not cover the cost of independent living, as it is considered a housing arrangement rather than a healthcare service.

What Are Life Plan Communities?

Life plan communities (also known as continuing care retirement communities, or CCRCs) are a unique option for older adults who want to plan by having access to multiple levels of care in one community. These communities offer a continuum of care—from independent living to assisted living, memory care, and skilled nursing care—all within the same location.

The Benefits of Life Plan Communities

- **Aging in Place:**
  One of the biggest advantages of a life plan community is that residents can age in place. This means they can start in an independent living apartment and seamlessly transition to assisted living or skilled nursing care as their health needs change, without

the stress of moving to a new location.

- **Comprehensive Services:**
  Life plan communities offer a wide range of services, including on-site healthcare, rehabilitation services, and access to specialists. This ensures that residents have consistent, high-quality care available to them as they age.

- **Social and Lifestyle Amenities:**
  Like independent living communities, life plan communities offer a variety of amenities and activities to help residents stay engaged and connected. These might include exercise classes, cultural outings, gardening, and educational programs. For many seniors, this offers a way to maintain an active, fulfilling lifestyle while also having access to care if needed.

- **Predictable Costs:**
  Many life plan communities operate on a fee-for-service model, where residents pay an entry fee and then a monthly fee for the services they use. This can provide cost predictability, as residents know that their long-term care needs will be covered without unexpected expenses.

What Do Life Plan Communities Cost?

Life plan communities typically require an upfront entry fee, which can range from $100,000 to $500,000 or more, depending on the size of the unit and the services offered. In addition to the entry fee, residents usually pay a monthly fee that covers housing, utilities, amenities, and some level of care. Monthly fees can range from $2,000 to $6,000 depending on the community and the level of care provided.

While these costs may seem high, many families find life plan communities to be a good investment because they offer peace of mind and eliminate the uncertainty of needing to move to different facilities as care needs increase. The continuum of care ensures that residents won't be forced to leave the community, even if their health deteriorates.

How to Pay for Life Plan Communities

The cost of life plan communities is generally covered by personal savings, retirement accounts, or the sale of a home. Some communities may accept long-term care insurance to cover healthcare services provided on-site. It's important to carefully review the financial terms of a life plan community before committing, as the entry fee and monthly costs vary widely.

Understanding 55+ Communities and Active Adult Living: How They Differ from Independent Living

When exploring housing options for seniors, **55+ communities** and **active adult living** often emerge as viable alternatives, especially for those who are still independent and want to maintain an active lifestyle. While these communities are sometimes seen as alternatives to **independent living (IL)**, they differ in terms of services, amenities, and the level of care provided.

Here's a breakdown of the key differences between these options to help you decide which is the best fit for your or your loved one's needs.

55+ Communities: Age-Restricted Living with a Focus on Independence

A **55+ community** is designed specifically for older adults. As the name implies, these communities are age-restricted, usually requiring at least one resident to be 55 or older, though some communities allow a certain percentage of younger residents, like spouses under 55.

Key Features of 55+ Communities:

- **Independent Lifestyle:** These communities cater to seniors who are still active and self-sufficient, without needing assistance with daily tasks or medical care.

- **Home Ownership or Rental Options:** Residents can typically choose from low-maintenance housing options, such as single-family homes, condominiums, or apartments. Services like lawn care and exterior maintenance are often included.

- **Social Opportunities:** A major appeal of 55+ communities is the social aspect. Amenities such as swimming pools, golf courses, fitness centers, and clubhouses provide spaces for socializing and organized activities like group trips, fitness programs, and community events.

- **Limited to No Health Services:** Unlike independent or assisted living, 55+ communities don't offer health or personal care services. Residents must arrange for outside help if needed.

Who Is a Good Fit for a 55+ Community?

- Active, independent seniors who want to live in a low-maintenance environment with peers of the same age.
- Those who enjoy social engagement and community activities.
- Individuals who do not require daily assistance or medical care.

Active Adult Communities: A Focus on an Active and Engaged Lifestyle

Similar to 55+ communities, **active adult communities** emphasize an active, healthy lifestyle. While also age-restricted, these communities focus on physical fitness, social engagement, and recreational activities more than traditional 55+ communities.

Key Features of Active Adult Communities:

- **Recreation-Oriented:** Extensive recreational facilities such as tennis courts, pickleball, walking trails, and fitness centers encourage residents to stay active with group sports, fitness classes, and wellness programs.

- **Lifestyle Focused:** Like 55+ communities, active adult living offers low-maintenance homes, allowing residents to focus on enjoying their retirement. Landscaping, exterior upkeep, and sometimes even housekeeping are handled by the community.

- **Resort-Style Living:** These communities often resemble resorts, offering luxury clubhouses, pools, and organized group activities such as yoga, art workshops, and day trips.

- **No On-Site Medical Care:** Residents are responsible for managing their own health care and must hire outside assistance if necessary.

Who Is a Good Fit for an Active Adult Community?

- Seniors who are physically active and want to maintain a fitness-focused lifestyle.
- Those looking for a resort-style living experience with recreational amenities.
- Individuals who are independent and do not require daily personal or medical care.

Independent Living (IL): A Supportive Environment with More Services

Independent living (IL) communities differ from 55+ and active adult communities by offering more services and support while allowing residents to maintain their independence. IL communities are designed for seniors who are mostly self-sufficient but may appreciate help with meals, housekeeping, and transportation.

Key Features of Independent Living:

- **Services Included:** IL communities offer services such as housekeeping, dining options, and transportation. These services are designed to reduce the burdens of home maintenance, cooking, and driving.
- **On-Site Staff:** Although IL doesn't provide medical care, there is usually staff available 24/7 for emergencies or assistance.
- **Meal Plans and Dining:** Most IL communities provide restaurant-style dining or meal plans, giving residents the option to enjoy prepared meals.
- **Social Activities:** Like 55+ and active adult communities, IL communities offer activities and fitness programs. However, the focus is on providing support while allowing seniors to maintain their independence.
- **Health and Wellness:** While direct medical care isn't provided, IL communities often have wellness programs or partner with home health services to bring in assistance when needed.

Who Is a Good Fit for Independent Living?

- Seniors who are independent but prefer some support with daily tasks such as meals, housekeeping, or transportation.
- Those who want to avoid the responsibilities of home ownership.

- Individuals who want a socially connected environment with the reassurance that help is available if needed.

Feature	55+ Communities	Active Adult Communities	Independent Living (IL)
Age Restriction	Typically 55+	Typically 55+	Generally 55+, may vary
Focus	Low-maintenance living, social activities	Active, fitness-focused lifestyle	Independence with services like meals and housekeeping
Home Ownership	Mostly home ownership or rentals	Mostly home ownership	Primarily rental apartments
Services Provided	Limited, no medical or personal care	Limited, no medical or personal care	Housekeeping, meals, trans-portation, emergency staff
Medical Care	None	None	None on-site, but assistance can be arranged
Amenities	Clubhouses, social activities	Extensive recreational amenities	Social activities, dining op-tions, support services
Ideal For	Independent seniors wanting low-maintenance living	Active seniors seeking recreation and fitness	Seniors seeking support services but valuing independence

Cost Comparison

55+ and Active Adult Communities: Costs vary widely but typically range from $1,500 to $3,500 per month for rentals, plus the cost of buying a home or condo if ownership is involved. These costs do not typically include services or meals.

Independent Living: Costs tend to range from $2,500 to $5,000 per month, often including rent, utilities, dining options, housekeeping, and transportation.

Which Option Is Right for Your Loved One?

Choosing between 55+ communities, active adult living, and independent living depends on your loved one's current needs, preferences, and future plans. If they are active, independent, and seeking social engagement in a low-maintenance setting, a 55+ or active adult community might be the best choice. However, if they want the added support of services like housekeeping and dining, **independent living** may be the better option.

The Gift of a Full Life

The decision to move a loved one into any form of congregate living—whether independent living, assisted living, or memory care—can be challenging. It's natural to feel the emotional weight of such a decision, but for seniors, it often represents the beginning of a new chapter. Moving into a community setting can transform their lives, providing social connections, engaging activities, and the peace of mind that comes from having the care and services they need.

For Marjorie, the first year of adjustment was difficult. But over time, she began to thrive. She wasn't just surviving anymore—she was living. She found new friends, rediscovered old hobbies, and felt a renewed sense of belonging in her community. Jane, too, found peace knowing her mother was safe, cared for, and most importantly—happy.

While the journey may be challenging, the reward is a life not just longer—but fuller.

Conclusion
Finding the Right Option

For seniors and their families, navigating the different types of senior living options—whether independent living or a life plan community—can feel overwhelming. However, these communities offer an incredible opportunity for seniors to live with independence, support, and connection.

Independent living is a great option for seniors who are looking for a simpler lifestyle without the worries of home maintenance and who want to stay socially active. Life plan communities, on the other hand, provide a sense of security for those who want to age in place, knowing that as their needs change, they will continue to be cared for within the same supportive community.

Both options provide more than just a place to live—they offer a chance to live fully, surrounded by friends and activities, with the support to enjoy life's later years in comfort and security. When considering these options, it's important to assess both current needs and future possibilities so you can find the best fit for your loved one's lifestyle and health.

Parent's Perspective

I've always been proud of my independence. For years, I've managed the house on my own—keeping up with the yard, cooking meals, running errands. But I'll admit, lately, things have been feeling a bit heavier. The house is quieter than it used to be, and more often than not, I find myself lonely. It's not that I can't take care of things; it's that some days I wonder if I still want to. The thought of moving, though, is daunting. This house holds so many memories. It's been my place of comfort for decades.

But as much as I cherish this place, I can't ignore the changes happening. The yard feels bigger, the stairs feel steeper, and I feel more isolated than I ever thought I would. I've been hearing more and more about independent living communities from my daughter, and while the idea seemed unsettling at first—like admitting I'm no longer capable, it's started to feel more like a possibility, even a relief.

I like the thought of letting go of the daily upkeep. I can imagine not having to worry about fixing the leaky faucet or shoveling snow. I could spend more time doing the things I actually enjoy, maybe getting back into some hobbies or joining activities with people my age. I miss that. I miss the conversations, the little social moments that were once part of my everyday life.

And the amenities sound great. I don't need help with personal care, at least not yet, but the idea of having someone around if I need them is comforting. I won't lie; the thought of having a meal prepared for me some nights sounds like a treat too. I've always loved to cook, but it's become more of a chore lately than a joy. Maybe, just maybe, it wouldn't be so bad to have the freedom to join others for dinner or relax knowing someone else is handling it.

The social aspect is what's pulling me in the most. I used to be so involved—bridge nights, volunteer groups, neighborhood gatherings—but as I've gotten older, I've lost touch with some of that. It would be nice to be part of a community again, to have a place where people are close by, where there's always something happening. It sounds like it could be fun—fitness classes, book clubs, group trips. It's the kind of engagement I didn't even realize I missed.

I guess the hardest part is accepting that this move isn't about giving up my independence but rather preserving it in a different way. I still want to live my life fully—I just don't want to do it alone or struggle with things that don't matter as much anymore. And as I think about the flexibility these places offer, like the option to transition into more care if I ever need it, it gives me peace of mind. I wouldn't have to move again; I could settle in knowing I'm covered for the long term.

I think, deep down, I know it's time for a change. Moving into an independent living community might be just what I need. It feels less like giving something up and more like opening the door to a new chapter—one where I can still be myself, but with a little extra support when I need it. The thought of having everything at my fingertips—activities, friends, help if I need it—makes me feel like I could not only maintain my independence but actually enhance it.

At the end of the day, this move isn't about leaving my life behind. It's about choosing a better way to live it, with fewer burdens and more joy. Maybe that's not such a bad thing after all.

Resources for Independent Living and Senior Housing Options

1. **LeadingAge**
   A national association of nonprofit organizations dedicated to providing senior services. They offer resources for independent living, continuing care retirement communities (CCRCs), and other senior housing options. Their website includes a "Find a Community" tool.
   » **Website:** leadingage.org

2. **National Center for Assisted Living (NCAL)**
   While NCAL focuses on assisted living, they offer valuable information for independent living and other senior housing options.
   » **Website:** ahcancal.org

3. **SeniorLiving.org – Independent Living Resource Guide**
   Provides a comprehensive guide to independent living communities, covering basics, tips on choosing the right community, and managing the costs.
   » **Website:** seniorliving.org

4. **The National Investment Center for Seniors Housing & Care (NIC)**
   NIC offers data and research on senior housing and care communities, including independent living and CCRCs.
   » **Website:** nic.org

5. **The International Council on Active Aging (ICAA)**
   Provides resources and advocacy for active aging, focusing on wellness programs and active lifestyles for older adults.
   » **Website:** icaa.cc

6. **55Places.com**
   An online guide to 55+ communities and active adult living, allowing users to search for communities by state, size, and amenities.
   » **Website:** 55places.com

7. **AARP – Moving to Independent Living**
   Offers a guide on choosing and transitioning into independent living communities, with practical advice on evaluating communities and budgeting.
   » **Website:** aarp.org

8. **Senior Housing Net**
   Helps families find senior living communities, including independent living, 55+ communities, and life plan communities.
   » **Website:** seniorhousingnet.com

9. **Continuing Care Retirement Communities (CCRC) Directory by Caring.com**
   A directory of CCRCs, with detailed descriptions, pricing information, and resident reviews.
   » **Website:** caring.com

Chapter 13
The Hidden Costs of Aging

When Diane first realized her father, Tom, needed more help than she could provide, she naively thought his savings and Medicare would be enough to cover whatever care he needed. But as Tom's health continued to decline, and she began looking into options like home care and assisted living, the reality hit hard: the cost of aging is astronomical. What started as a few hours of in-home care quickly spiraled into a maze of monthly bills, unexpected expenses, and limitations on what insurance would cover. Diane felt overwhelmed, underprepared, and worried about how long her father's resources would last.

Diane's story is one that many families know all too well. The financial realities of caring for an aging parent can be devastating if you're not prepared. The costs aren't always visible at first, but as needs increase, the expenses pile up. Home care, assisted living, memory care, nursing homes—each option has its price, and families are shocked to learn that most of these costs aren't covered by Medicare or private insurance.

This chapter aims to provide a compassionate but realistic look at the hidden costs of aging and the resources available to help. By understanding what lies ahead, you can better prepare for the financial demands of caring for your loved one—and yourself.

A Breakdown of the Costs: What You Can Expect

As discussed throughout this book, the costs of senior care vary widely depending on the type of care needed, where you live, and the level of services required. Here's a breakdown of the common options:

Home Care

- **Cost:** According to Genworth's "Cost of Care Survey 2023," home care typically costs between $20 and $30 per hour, depending on where you live and the level of care provided. A full-time home health aide can cost between $4,000 and $5,500 per month.

- **Services:** Home care includes help with daily tasks like bathing, dressing, and meal preparation. Home care aides are also trained to provide basic medical care, such as medication management or physical therapy.

- **When It's a Good Fit:** Home care is ideal for seniors who want to remain at home but need assistance with daily activities.

Assisted Living

- **Cost:** The national average for assisted living is around $4,500 per month, but this can range from $3,000 to over $7,000 depending on the location and amenities.

- **Services:** Assisted living communities provide housing, meals, and help with personal care. Most communities offer activities, transportation, and 24-hour supervision, but they do not provide intensive medical care.

- **When It's a Good Fit:** Assisted living is suitable for seniors who need help with daily activities but do not require around-the-clock medical care.

Memory Care

- **Cost:** Genworth Financial's 2023 Cost of Care Survey found that memory care is more expensive, typically ranging from $5,000 to $10,000 per month. This higher cost is due to the specialized care and security provided for individuals with Alzheimer's or other forms of dementia.

- **Services:** Memory care includes 24/7 supervision, specialized staff trained in dementia care, and secure environments to prevent wandering.

- **When It's a Good Fit:** Memory care is necessary for seniors with significant cognitive decline who may require constant supervision and specialized care.

Skilled Nursing

- **Cost:** The same Genworth Financial "Cost of Care Survey 2023" found that skilled nursing homes are the most expensive, with costs averaging around $8,000 to $9,000 per month. In some areas, this can rise to over $10,000.

- **Services:** These facilities provide 24/7 medical care, rehabilitation, and personal care for seniors who need constant monitoring due to serious health conditions.

- **When It's a Good Fit:** Skilled nursing is necessary for seniors who require full-time medical care and supervision, often due to chronic illnesses or after major surgeries.

Independent Living

- **Cost:** The SeniorLiving.org "Cost of Independent Living (2023)" found that independent living communities cost between $2,500 and $5,000 per month, depending on the location and amenities.

- **Services:** These communities offer housing with limited services, such as housekeeping, dining, and social activities. Medical care is typically not included, but residents can hire outside help if needed.

- **When It's a Good Fit:** Independent living is ideal for seniors who are still active and don't need assistance with daily tasks but want the convenience of a community setting.

Active Adult and 55+ Communities

- **Cost:** According to SeniorLiving.org's "Cost of 55+ Communities," these communities usually involve either purchasing a home, condo, or renting. Monthly fees range from $1,500 to $3,500. Homeowners may also pay HOA fees for maintenance and shared amenities.

- **Services:** These communities are geared towards healthy, active seniors. They offer social activities, fitness centers, and recreational amenities but no medical or personal care services.

- **When It's a Good Fit:** Best for seniors who want to downsize and enjoy an active, social retirement without the worry of home maintenance.

Life Plan Communities (CCRCs)

- **Cost:** Life plan communities, or Continuing Care Retirement Communities (CCRCs), require an upfront entry fee ranging from $100,000 to $500,000 or more, plus monthly fees that range from $2,000 to $6,000, according to the National Investment Center for Seniors Housing & Care (NIC).

- **Services:** These communities offer a continuum of care, from independent living to assisted living, memory care, and skilled nursing, allowing residents to age in place as their needs change.

- **When It's a Good Fit:** Life plan communities are a good option for seniors who want to plan and ensure they will have access to all levels of care in one place.

What Medicare, Medicaid, and Private Insurance Do—and Don't—Cover

Families mistakenly assume that Medicare or private insurance will cover most long-term care costs, but the reality is that these programs offer limited assistance when it comes to senior care.

Medicare

- **What It Covers:** Medicare primarily covers short-term medical care, such as hospital stays, rehabilitation, and limited home health care following a hospital stay. Medicare may also cover a limited number of days in a skilled nursing facility for rehabilitation after a hospital stay of at least three days.

- **What It Doesn't Cover:** Medicare does not cover long-term care, including the costs associated with home care, assisted living, memory care, or long-term stays in nursing homes.

Medicaid

- **What It Covers**: Medicaid is a state and federally funded program that covers long-term care for low-income individuals. Medicaid will cover the costs of a skilled nursing facility or, in some states, in-home care and assisted living, but eligibility is based on income and assets. Seniors often need to spend down their assets to qualify.

- **What It Doesn't Cover:** Medicaid does not cover all senior living options, particularly those like independent living or life plan communities. Coverage varies from state to state, and not all communities accept Medicaid.

Private Insurance

- What It Covers: Private health insurance typically focuses on short-term medical needs. While it may cover rehabilitation or temporary stays in skilled nursing facilities, it does not cover long-term care.

- What It Doesn't Cover: Long-term care, including assisted living or memory care, is not typically covered under private health insurance policies.

How to Find Out If Your Parent Has Long-Term Care Insurance

- **Check Their Financial Records:** Long-term care insurance policies are usually purchased separately from traditional health insurance. Review your parent's financial documents, insurance policies, or annual statements to see if they have long-term care coverage.

- **Contact Their Insurance Agent:** If your parent worked with a financial planner or insurance agent, they may have records of whether a policy was purchased. Don't hesitate to reach out to their previous agent or any financial professional they worked with.

- **Ask Your Parent:** While this can be a difficult conversation, it's important to ask your parent directly if they remember purchasing long-term care insurance. Many seniors buy these policies when they're younger and healthier but forget about them as the years go by.

Why You Should Consider Long-Term Care Insurance for Yourself

As a caregiver, you are witnessing the tremendous financial burden aging can place on a family. While long-term care insurance can be expensive, purchasing a policy for yourself now—while you're younger and healthier—can be a wise investment for your future. The sooner you purchase a policy, the lower the premiums will be.

Long-term care insurance offers peace of mind, ensuring that when you need assistance in the future, the financial burden won't fall entirely on your loved ones. It's an important consideration in planning for your own aging process and avoiding the financial strain that so many families face today.

Conclusion:
Navigating the Hidden Costs of Aging

The costs of aging are often hidden until families are thrust into a caregiving role and realize how overwhelming the financial demands can be. Whether it's home care, assisted living, memory care, or skilled nursing, the price of care can quickly drain savings and put families in a difficult position. Understanding what different options cost and what is—and isn't—covered by insurance is the first step in making informed decisions.

Father's Response to "The Hidden Costs of Aging"

I never thought I'd find myself in this position—being the one who needed help. All those years of working hard, saving money, and planning for retirement, I thought I'd be prepared for anything. But what they don't tell you is just how expensive it is to grow old. Sure, I knew healthcare could get pricey, but the costs of day-to-day care? That was a rude awakening.

I used to be proud of my independence. I could take care of myself, handle my own affairs, and stay on top of things. But after the falls and the confusion started to creep in, I realized that I needed more help than I could manage alone. Diane, my daughter, stepped in, thinking my savings and Medicare would be enough to cover things. I thought so too. Turns out, we were both wrong.

The costs started piling up faster than we could've imagined. What began as a few hours of help each week quickly spiraled into something more. Home care, assisted living options, and now talks of memory care—it all felt overwhelming. I could see the worry on Diane's face as she tried to figure out how long my savings would last. I felt guilty. I didn't want to be a burden to her, to anyone really.

Medicare, which I always believed would take care of me, barely scratched the surface. It only covered short-term medical needs, but the daily care, help with getting dressed, eating, and even remembering where I'd put my keys—that wasn't included. It was a slap in the face to realize that so much of what I needed wasn't covered. And the idea of Medicaid? It was hard to process. The thought of having to spend down everything I'd worked for just to qualify felt unfair.

Diane talked to me about long-term care insurance, but I didn't get one of those policies when I was younger. Like most folks, I thought I wouldn't need it. I thought I'd be okay. Now, I can see the strain this is putting on my family, and I can't help but wonder if I should've planned differently. It's easy to look back and wish you'd made different choices, but at the time, you just don't think you'll end up needing so much help.

There's a lot of shame wrapped up in this, too. Having to rely on others, watching your savings disappear, and knowing that your family is stressed because of you—it's tough. But I'm also grateful. Grateful for Diane's patience, for the care I'm receiving, even if it costs more than I ever expected. And now, as I look ahead, all I can hope is that my kids don't have to go through the same thing with me. I hope they plan better, maybe consider long-term care insurance while they still can.

Aging is expensive in ways I never saw coming, and it's humbling to realize how little control you have over that. But if there's one thing I've learned, it's that you can't face it alone. It's okay to ask for help, even when it's hard. It's okay to admit that you didn't plan for everything. And most importantly, it's okay to lean on your family because in the end, they're the ones who are going to carry you through this.

1. **Genworth Cost of Care Survey**
   One of the most comprehensive resources for understanding the costs of senior care across the U.S., providing average costs for home care, assisted living, memory care, and nursing homes in different regions.
   » **Website:** https://www.genworth.com/aging-and-you/finances/cost-of-care.html

2. **The American Association for Long-Term Care Insurance (AALTCI)**
   Offers resources on long-term care insurance, including how to purchase a policy, file claims, and understand coverage options.
   » **Website:** https://www.aaltci.org/

3. **ElderCare Locator - Financial Assistance for Seniors**
   Helps families find local resources, including financial assistance programs, elder law attorneys, and state-specific Medicaid options.
   » **Website:** https://eldercare.acl.gov/Public/Index.aspx
   » **Phone:** 800-677-1116

4. **Veterans Aid and Attendance Benefit**
   Provides financial assistance for long-term care, including home care, assisted living, and nursing home care for veterans and their spouses.
   » **Website:** https://www.va.gov/pension/aid-attendance-housebound/

5. **National Council on Aging (NCOA) - BenefitsCheckUp**
   Helps seniors find state and federal benefits that can offset the cost of aging, such as housing assistance and healthcare subsidies.
   » **Website:** https://www.benefitscheckup.org/

6. **Medicare Interactive - Long-Term Care Costs**
   Provides information on what Medicare covers in terms of long-term care, along with strategies for using Medicare alongside other financial resources.
   » **Website:** https://www.medicareinteractive.org/get-answers/medicare-covered-services/limited-medicare-coverage-long-term-care-services/medicare-and-long-term-care-basics

7. **National Elder Law Foundation (NELF)**
   Certifies elder law attorneys who specialize in legal issues affecting seniors, such as Medicaid planning and long-term care costs.
   » **Website:** https://nelf.org/

8. **State Health Insurance Assistance Programs (SHIP)**
   Offers free, one-on-one counseling to Medicare beneficiaries and their families, helping them navigate Medicare, Medicaid, and long-term care insurance options.
   » **Website:** https://www.shiphelp.org/

9. **Family Caregiver Alliance - Financial & Legal Issues in Caregiving**
   Offers guides to financial and legal issues for caregivers, covering Medicaid planning, long-term care insurance, and asset protection.
   » **Website:** https://www.caregiver.org/caregiver-resources/caring-for-another/legal-and-financial-planning/

Summary

Aging brings emotional and financial costs that can catch families by surprise. This chapter uncovers the realities of medical bills, care expenses, and the long-term financial impact. By planning ahead and exploring resources, you can better protect your parent's well-being and preserve their legacy.

CRACK THE CODE

Chapter 14
Paying for Care

When Janet's father, George, began showing signs of dementia, she found herself suddenly thrust into the role of caregiver. While she knew he needed help, she had no idea how they would afford the care he required. George had always been frugal, but as Janet went through his finances, she realized his savings wouldn't last long. Overwhelmed by the maze of care options and unsure where to turn, Janet felt lost. How do you pay for care when it seems out of reach?

Janet's situation is one that many families face. Understanding how to pay for senior care can feel like navigating a financial minefield. VA benefits, Social Security, and other financial assistance programs can help, but they often don't cover everything. What happens if your parent has little to no savings? This chapter will break down common financial resources, offer guidance on using your loved one's assets wisely, and provide hope for those feeling overwhelmed by the costs of care.

VA Benefits, Social Security, and Other Financial Assistance Programs

There are several programs designed to help seniors pay for care, but many families either aren't aware of them or don't know how to access them. Here are the most commonly available resources:

VA Benefits

If your parent is a veteran, they may qualify for Veterans Affairs (VA) benefits, which can significantly help pay for long-term care.

- **Aid and Attendance:** This benefit provides additional monthly financial assistance to veterans (and their surviving spouses) who need help with daily activities like dressing, bathing, or eating. It can be used to pay for home care, assisted living, or nursing home care.

- **Eligibility:** To qualify, your parent must have served at least 90 days of active duty, with at least one day during wartime, and must need assistance with daily living. There are also financial eligibility requirements.

- **How to Apply:** Contact your local VA office or a veteran's service organization for help with the application process. The process can take time, but the benefits can ease the financial burden of care.
    - » **Website:** Veterans Aid and Attendance Benefit https://www.va.gov/pension/aid-attendance-housebound/

Social Security

Social Security alone won't cover the full cost of long-term care, but it provides a crucial income stream to help cover monthly expenses.

- **How it Works:** Social Security payments are based on your parent's work history. The amount they receive depends on how long they worked and how much they earned. These payments can help cover the cost of home care, independent living, or other senior care services.

- **Supplemental Security Income (SSI):** If your parent has limited income and resources, they may qualify for SSI, a federal program that provides financial assistance for basic needs like housing, food, and medical care.
    - » **Website:** Social Security Administration https://www.ssa.gov/ssi

Medicaid

For seniors with limited income and assets, Medicaid can be a critical resource. While Medicare covers short-term medical needs, Medicaid can cover long-term care services, including nursing home care and, in some states, assisted living or home health care.

- **Eligibility:** Medicaid eligibility varies by state, but typically requires that your parent has a low income and few assets. Seniors often need to "spend down" their savings to meet Medicaid's eligibility limits.

- **How to Apply:** Contact your state's Medicaid office to learn more about eligibility and how to apply.
    » **Website:** https://www.ssa.https://www.ssa.gov/apply/ssi/apply/ssi

Other Financial Assistance Programs

There are additional programs that may help your parent cover care costs:

- **State Assistance Programs:** Many states offer programs like Home and Community-Based Services (HCBS), which provide financial support for home care, transportation, and meal programs.

- **Nonprofit Organizations:** Groups like the Family Caregiver Alliance and the National Council on Aging offer grants or financial aid to help cover the costs of care.
    » **Website:** Family Caregiver Alliance https://www.caregiver.org
    » **Website:** National Council on Aging https://www.ncoa.org

Using Your Parent's Assets: Navigating the Financial Web of Aging

If your parent has savings or assets such as a home or retirement accounts, these resources can help pay for their care. However, managing these assets involves difficult decisions and careful planning.

Using Savings and Investments

If your parent has savings, retirement accounts, or other investments, these can be used to pay for care. However, the cost of long-term care can quickly deplete savings, so it's important to have a clear plan.

- **Withdrawals from Retirement Accounts:** If your parent has a 401(k) or IRA, funds may need to be withdrawn to cover care. Be mindful of tax implications and potential penalties for early withdrawals.

- **Liquidating Investments:** Stocks, bonds, or other investments can be sold to pay for care. However, it's crucial to consider market conditions and tax consequences before liquidating assets.

Selling the Family Home

For many seniors, the family home is their largest asset. While selling it can be emotional, it's often a necessary step to finance long-term care.

- **Downsizing or Selling:** If your parent no longer needs a large home, selling it and downsizing can free up significant funds to cover care costs.

- **Reverse Mortgages:** A reverse mortgage allows your parent to access the equity in their home while continuing to live there. This

can provide a steady income stream to pay for home care, but be aware of high fees and the risk of losing the home after the loan becomes due.
- » **Website:** Consumer Financial Protection Bureau on Reverse Mortgages https://www.consumerfinance.gov/ask-cfpb/what-is-a-reverse-mortgage-en-224/

Navigating Financial Documents

Managing your parent's assets often requires gathering and organizing complex financial documents. Here are some steps to help:

- **Gather Financial Documents:** Collect all financial records, including bank statements, retirement accounts, insurance policies, and tax returns.

- **Consult a Financial Planner:** Working with a financial planner or elder law attorney can help ensure your parent's assets are used wisely and that they have the funds needed for long-term care.
  - » **Website:** National Academy of Elder Law Attorneys https://www.naela.org

What to Do If Your Parent Has No Savings or Insurance: Alternative Resources

If your parent has little to no savings or long-term care insurance, paying for care can seem impossible. Fortunately, there are alternative resources available.

Medicaid

As mentioned earlier, Medicaid can be a lifeline for seniors with limited income. It covers nursing home care and, in some states, assisted living

or in-home care services.
  » Website: Medicaid.gov

PACE (Program of All-Inclusive Care for the Elderly)

PACE is a Medicare and Medicaid program that provides comprehensive medical and social services for seniors who need a high level of care but want to remain at home.

- **Eligibility:** PACE is available to seniors who qualify for nursing home care but prefer to receive services in their homes or communities.

- **Services Covered:** PACE covers a wide range of services, including medical care, home health services, adult day care, meals, and transportation.
  » **Website:** PACE https://www.npaonline.org

Nonprofit Assistance

Nonprofit organizations like Meals on Wheels, the National Council on Aging, and other local groups often provide financial aid or discounted services for seniors.

  » **Website:** Meals on Wheels America https://www.mealsonwheelsamerica.org
  » **Website:** The National Council https://www.ncoa.org/

Family Support

If resources are tight, family members may need to contribute to the cost of care. While these conversations can be difficult, bringing siblings or other relatives into the discussion about finances can help share the responsibility.

A Story of Hope: Finding the Right Resources

When Janet's father, George, first started needing help, she felt completely lost. With little savings and no long-term care insurance, Janet didn't know how they would manage. But after talking to a veteran's service officer, she discovered George was eligible for VA Aid and Attendance benefits, which provided over $2,000 a month to help with his care. Janet also applied for Medicaid, which would cover the cost of a skilled nursing facility when George's needs became more intensive.

While the process wasn't easy, Janet found that there were more resources available than she had initially thought. With careful planning, she was able to ensure her father received the care he needed without depleting all his assets.

Conclusion
Facing the Financial Reality with Hope

Paying for senior care is one of the most daunting challenges families face. Whether your parent has savings or is relying on programs like Medicaid, knowing what resources are available—and how to access them—can make a world of difference. VA benefits, Social Security, Medicaid, and nonprofit organizations can help bridge the gap, while careful management of your parent's assets can ensure their financial stability for the long term.

While the costs of aging are real, so are the options for help. With the right planning, you can navigate this difficult time with confidence and hope.

Father's Response to the Hidden Cost of Aging

I have to admit that facing the costs of aging—it's a lot to take in. I've always been careful with my money, tried to save, live within my means, and thought I'd have enough set aside. But when you get to this point, the reality hits—medical care, long-term care, and even basic support services cost a fortune. It's overwhelming.

I never expected to find myself needing so much help. I used to think that with Social Security and the money I saved, I'd be set for life. But now I see how quickly those savings can disappear. Reading about how even something like home care, which seems basic enough, can cost thousands each month is humbling. And then there's the realization that Medicare doesn't cover most of it—that's a shock. I didn't know all of this before now, and I can only imagine how hard it is for my daughter Janet to figure it all out while worrying about me.

What I'm feeling now is a mix of fear, guilt, and maybe even a little frustration. I never wanted to be a financial burden on my family. I worked hard all my life so that wouldn't happen, but now I'm seeing the costs add up, and it feels out of my control. There's fear because I don't know how long my savings will last or what will happen when they run out. Will I end up having to sell the home that means so much to me? Will Medicaid be enough?

At the same time, I feel grateful that Janet is finding resources I didn't even know about, like the VA benefits. I served, but I never thought about how those benefits could come into play now. It's a bit of a relief knowing that things like Aid and Attendance could provide some financial assistance. I'm still processing it all, and while I hate the idea of my daughter having to take on this responsibility, I also trust her and am thankful she's helping me navigate this complicated web of aging and finances.

It's tough to accept, but I know that, in the end, I need to let go of some of that control and rely on the resources that are available and on Janet to make sure I'm cared for without draining everything I've worked for. It's about coming to terms with the fact that aging isn't just physically challenging; it's financially overwhelming, but there are options—and I've got to hope we can find the right ones.

Additional Resources

- **Veterans Aid and Attendance Benefit**
  This benefit offers financial support to veterans or their surviving spouses who need help with daily activities like dressing or bathing.
  - » **Website:** https://www.va.gov/pension/aid-attendance-housebound/

- **PACE (Program of All-Inclusive Care for the Elderly)**
  PACE provides comprehensive medical and social services to seniors who qualify for nursing home care but prefer to remain at home.
  - » **Website:** https://www.npaonline.org/pace-you

- **Medicaid and Medicaid Waivers**
  Medicaid can provide coverage for long-term care, including nursing homes, and in some states, in-home or assisted living care.
  - » **Website:** Medicaid and Medicaid Waivers

- **National Council on Aging**
  This organization helps seniors find financial support and resources to assist with the costs of aging.
  - » **Website:** https://www.ncoa.org

- **Family Caregiver Alliance**
  Offers financial assistance resources and guides on managing long-term care costs for caregivers.
  » **Website:** https://www.caregiver.org

Summary

Paying for senior care can feel daunting, but resources are available to help lighten the load. This chapter explores financial assistance options, from government programs to veterans' benefits, and offers practical advice for navigating the maze of costs. With knowledge and preparation, you can create a plan that supports your parent's needs without unnecessary stress.

Chapter 15
Final Preparations End-of-Life Care and Hospice

When Susan's father, Bill, was diagnosed with terminal cancer, the news came like a sudden storm. The doctors told her there was nothing more they could do except manage his symptoms and keep him comfortable. But what did that even mean? Susan wasn't prepared for the weight of those words. She wasn't ready to face the reality that her father, the man who had been her rock for so long, was nearing the end of his life. She felt lost and overwhelmed, unsure of what decisions to make or how to ensure her father was cared for in his final days.

One of the doctors mentioned hospice care, but Susan was hesitant. Didn't that mean giving up? Would her father think she was abandoning hope? These questions swirled in her mind. But as Bill's condition worsened, Susan realized she couldn't do it all alone. The pain he was in, the sleepless nights—it was too much. That's when she made the difficult but compassionate decision to bring in hospice.

For families, the realization that a loved one is approaching the end of their life is one of the hardest things to face. Most of us are unprepared for what that means, both practically and emotionally. Hospice care can be an incredible source of support during this time, offering not only medical care but also emotional and spiritual comfort. This chapter will help you understand what hospice is, when to consider it, and how to navigate this deeply difficult period with as much grace and peace as possible.

When to Consider Hospice Care

It's often difficult to know when the right time is to consider hospice care. Many families wait too long, fearing that choosing hospice means giving up on their loved one. However, hospice is not about giving up—it's about shifting the focus from curative treatments to comfort and quality of life for the time that remains.

Hospice care is designed for people with a terminal illness and a life expectancy of six months or less, though patients can remain on hospice longer if needed. The goal of hospice is not to cure the illness but to manage pain, relieve symptoms, and provide emotional and spiritual support to both the patient and their family.

I vividly recall the care and comfort hospice brought to our family when my mother-in-law was dying. There was an incredible sense of calm amid the storm of emotion, fear, and confusion. It was as if the energy in the room shifted for everyone, including my mother-in-law, who found peace as her passing approached.

Signs It May Be Time to Consider Hospice:

- **Frequent Hospital Visits:** If your loved one is frequently hospitalized or making multiple trips to the emergency room, hospice care may help manage symptoms more effectively at home.

- **Decline in Physical Health:** If your loved one is losing weight, becoming weaker, or struggling with daily tasks such as eating, bathing, or walking, hospice may provide the support they need to maintain dignity and comfort.

- **Increased Pain and Suffering:** If treatments are no longer improving their quality of life and they're in significant pain or discomfort, hospice can focus on pain management and symptom relief.

- **Doctor's Recommendation:** If doctors have indicated that treatments are no longer effective or that your parent's condition is terminal, it may be time to consider hospice care.

For Susan, shifting from "fighting" the disease to focusing on her father's comfort was a difficult but necessary transition. Once hospice stepped in, Bill's pain was managed, and Susan was able to spend meaningful time with him, rather than focusing on managing his needs.

What Hospice Provides and How It Supports Families

Hospice care goes beyond managing physical symptoms—it provides holistic care, supporting the emotional, spiritual, and practical needs of both the patient and their family. Hospice can take place in the home, hospital, or hospice facility, depending on the patient's preferences.

What Hospice Provides:

- **Pain and Symptom Management:** Hospice focuses on keeping the patient comfortable by managing pain, nausea, shortness of breath, and other symptoms.

- **In-Home Care:** Hospice offers in-home nursing care, medical equipment like hospital beds or oxygen, and medications to manage symptoms. Nurses and aides regularly visit to check on the patient.

- **Emotional Support:** Social workers and counselors provide emotional support to both the patient and their family, helping them cope with the reality of saying goodbye.

- **Spiritual Care:** Hospice programs offer chaplains or spiritual counselors who can help the patient and family find peace and meaning during the end-of-life process.

- **Respite Care for Families:** Hospice provides respite care, offering short-term care in a facility to give caregivers a break.

- **Bereavement Support:** After the patient passes, hospice offers grief counseling and bereavement support to family members, helping them navigate their loss.

For Susan, hospice was a lifeline. The hospice nurses cared for Bill with compassion, managing his pain so he could rest peacefully. They provided invaluable emotional support, helping Susan cope with her feelings of guilt, sadness, and helplessness.

Emotional and Spiritual Preparation for Saying Goodbye

There's no way to fully prepare for the moment you have to say goodbye to a parent. The emotional toll can feel overwhelming, especially when the end follows a long illness. But as difficult as it is, there are ways to approach this time with intention, allowing you to make the most of the days or weeks that remain.

Acknowledge the Grief

Grieving doesn't begin when a loved one passes away—it often starts when you realize their time is limited. Allow yourself to feel and process your emotions. Anticipatory grief, sadness, anger, and even relief that their suffering will end are all valid feelings.

Focus on Meaningful Time

One of the gifts of hospice care is that it allows families to focus on quality time rather than the logistics of medical care. Use this time to say the things that need to be said. Share stories, reminisce, and express your love. Sometimes, simply sitting together is enough.

Toward the end, Bill could no longer speak, but Susan sat by his side, holding his hand, reading him favorite passages from books, and playing his favorite music. These moments of connection became cherished memories for her.

Spiritual and Emotional Reflection

End-of-life care often brings deep questions about meaning and legacy. Hospice chaplains or spiritual counselors can offer guidance, helping you and your loved one find peace and comfort during this emotional time. For Susan, the hospice chaplain provided solace, helping her explore her feelings of loss and reminding her that it was okay to feel overwhelmed.

Prepare for the End

The final days of life can be difficult, but being prepared for what to expect can help reduce anxiety. Hospice staff will help guide you when the end is near, ensuring your loved one remains comfortable. In the last hours, patients become less responsive, their breathing changes, and they may become agitated. Hospice nurses will be there to guide you through these stages.

For Susan, the end came peacefully. Bill passed away at home, in his bed, surrounded by the people who loved him most. As difficult as it was, Susan was grateful for the care and support hospice provided, knowing that her father was treated with dignity and care in his final moments.

Conclusion:
Finding Peace in the Final Goodbye

The decision to bring in hospice care is never easy. It's a recognition that your loved one's time is limited, which can feel unbearable. However, it is a compassionate choice—one that shifts the focus to comfort, peace, and dignity in their final days. Hospice provides families with the gift of time, allowing them to say goodbye, reflect, and simply be present.

For Susan, those final days were hard but also filled with love, connection, and peace. Though the pain of losing her father was profound, she found comfort in knowing that his last moments were spent in the presence of those who loved him most.

What Dad Might Say if Able

As I reflect on this chapter, it brings up a lot of emotions I've been trying to push aside. I've always thought of myself as capable, strong enough to handle anything life throws my way. But the truth is, nothing really prepares you for the idea that your time might be running out. It's strange to think about hospice and what it means for me and my family. Part of me is scared because it feels like admitting that the end is near, but another part of me feels some relief. Maybe it's not about giving up—maybe it's about choosing peace.

I've spent my whole life looking after my family, making sure things were in order. The thought of letting go of control doesn't sit well with me, but I understand now that it's okay. Hospice could mean that I don't have to fight anymore—that my pain and struggles don't have to be the focus. I want to be comfortable. I want my family to have more time to just be with me, instead of worrying about all the details of my care.

The hardest part of all this isn't for me—it's thinking about what this means for my family. I don't want them to feel like they're losing hope.

If hospice can give them emotional support and guide them through this, maybe they'll be able to look back and remember those final moments without so much pain. I want them to have peace with it too.

I realize how important it is to focus on the time I have left. I still want to make memories with the people I love, share stories, and laugh together. I don't want those last moments to be filled with fear or confusion. If hospice can help me be more present and comfortable, I think I'm ready to embrace it. It's not about giving up—it's about making sure the time I have left is filled with the love and connection that really matters.

Resources for Final Preparation

- **National Resource Center on Supportive Housing and Home Modification**
  This organization helps seniors and caregivers find financial assistance for home modifications that support aging in place, such as grab bars, ramps, and mobility improvements.
  » **Website:** https://homemods.org

- **Area Agencies on Aging (AAA)**
  Local AAAs provide information on financial assistance programs, state-funded options for in-home care, meal services, and transportation.
  » **Website:** https://eldercare.acl.gov/Public/Index.aspx

- **BenefitsCheckUp**
  An initiative by the National Council on Aging, BenefitsCheckUp helps families find federal and state assistance programs that cover costs associated with long-term care and home modifications.
  » **Website:** https://www.benefitscheckup.org

- **Life Care Funding**
  This organization helps families convert life insurance policies into funds for long-term care, providing immediate financial support for home care, assisted living, or nursing home care.
  » **Website:** https://www.lifecarefunding.com

- **Eldercare Financial Resource Locator**
  A comprehensive guide that helps families explore various methods for paying for senior care, including veteran benefits, Medicaid planning, reverse mortgages, and annuities.
  » **Website**: https://www.payingforseniorcare.com

- **Long-Term Care Insurance Association (LTCIA)**
  The LTCIA provides tools and resources for understanding long-term care insurance options and helps families review policies to determine coverage for senior care services.
  » **Website:** https://www.aaltci.org

- **National PACE Association (Program of All-Inclusive Care for the Elderly)**
  PACE provides comprehensive medical and social services for seniors who prefer to receive care at home but require a high level of care.
  » **Website:** https://www.npaonline.org

- **AARP Reverse Mortgage Counseling**
  AARP offers reverse mortgage counseling services, helping seniors determine if a reverse mortgage is a good financial decision to cover the costs of aging in place.
  » **Website:** https://www.aarp.org/money/credit-loans-debt/reverse_mortgages

- **Pension Rights Center**
  This organization provides free legal assistance to help seniors claim pensions and retirement benefits, which can be used to help pay for long-term care.
  » **Website:** https://www.pensionrights.org

- **National Association of Professional Geriatric Care Managers (NAPGCM)**
  NAPGCM members offer professional advice on managing a senior's finances, healthcare, and living arrangements, including navigating long-term care costs.
  » **Website:** https://www.aginglifecare.org

Chapter 16

Proactively Preparing for Your Own Journey into Aging

As we come to the end of this book, I want to take a moment to reflect on the journey we've taken together. If you've made it this far, you've been walking a difficult road—caring for an aging parent or loved one, grappling with the emotional, physical, and financial challenges that come with that responsibility. You've learned about the facets of caregiving, from navigating the healthcare maze to making end-of-life decisions, and I hope this book has provided clarity, comfort, and guidance along the way.

But now, I want to shift the focus to you and your future. While much of this book has been about caring for others, this final chapter is about the most important thing you can do moving forward—proactively preparing for your own aging journey. It's about ensuring that your children, spouse, or loved ones don't have to go through the same struggles you've faced and about giving yourself the gift of peace of mind knowing that when the time comes, your plans are in place.

Learning from Experience

As you reflect on the experience of caring for your loved one, you've likely realized how incredibly difficult it is to manage the unexpected. Much of the stress and confusion that comes with caregiving stems from not knowing what your loved one would have wanted or being unsure about how to manage their financial, legal, and medical needs.

The emotional burden of making decisions on their behalf—while also trying to come to terms with their decline—can be overwhelming.

For caregivers, the hardest part is feeling unprepared. You're suddenly thrust into a world of complicated paperwork, medical jargon, and emotional turmoil, all while trying to do the best for someone you love. But it doesn't have to be this way. By learning from the challenges you've faced, you can prepare differently for your own aging, making it easier for those who will care for you someday.

Why Proactive Planning is Essential

One of the most important lessons explored in this book is that uncertainty leads to stress. When there's no plan in place—no clear direction about how your loved one would have wanted to live their final years—caregivers are left guessing. They're left managing not only the practical aspects of care but also the emotional weight of "what if?"

By proactively planning for your own aging, you remove that uncertainty. You take the guesswork out of the equation, allowing your loved ones to focus on what truly matters—spending quality time with you and providing the care you need without the added stress of making difficult decisions on their own.

Steps to Take: Planning for Your Own Future

So, what does it look like to prepare for your own journey into aging? It's about making thoughtful, intentional decisions now—while you are still healthy and capable—so that your family has a clear path to follow when the time comes.

Create a Will and Advance Directives

One of the most important steps in planning for your future is to create a will and advance healthcare directives. These documents ensure that your wishes are followed, both in terms of how your assets are distributed and what kind of medical care you want to receive if you are unable to make those decisions yourself.

- **Your Will:** A will outlines how your estate—your money, property, and belongings—will be divided after you pass away. It also allows you to name an executor, the person responsible for carrying out your wishes.

- **Healthcare Directives:** Advance directives, including a living will and durable power of attorney for healthcare, ensure that your medical preferences are known and respected. These documents outline your preferences for care, including life-sustaining treatments, and appoint someone you trust to make healthcare decisions on your behalf if you are unable.

For more information, you can use the American Bar Association's Guide to Wills and Trusts.

Organize Your Financial and Legal Documents

Another way to prepare is by ensuring your financial and legal documents are organized and easily accessible. These include:

- Bank accounts and investment portfolios
- Retirement accounts (such as IRAs or 401(k)s)
- Life insurance policies
- Property deeds or titles
- Any other legal agreements or contracts

Having these documents in order will save your family from the stress of managing your financial affairs when they are already dealing with the emotional impact of your decline or passing.

Long-Term Care Plans

One of the most difficult aspects of aging is the potential need for long-term care, whether that's home care, assisted living, or memory care. While no one can predict their future needs, you can prepare by looking into long-term care insurance or other financial resources that will help cover the costs of care.

Consider:

- Researching long-term care insurance: If you're still relatively young and healthy, it may be worth investing in a policy that can cover the costs of long-term care. The American Association for Long-Term Care Insurance offers detailed information on this option. https://www.aaltci.org

- Discussing living options: Consider where you would want to live if you could no longer live independently at home. Would you prefer a 55+ community, independent living, or assisted living if your health declines? Share your preferences with your family so they can honor your wishes.

Have Open Conversations with Your Loved Ones

The most important step is to have open, honest conversations with your family about your wishes. By discussing your plans now, you give them the opportunity to ask questions, understand your preferences, and feel confident they are following your wishes when the time comes.

This conversation can be difficult, but it is incredibly freeing—for both you and your family. It removes the burden of uncertainty and gives them the peace of knowing they are honoring your legacy.

The Peace of Mind That Comes with Preparation

For Sarah, after her mother passed away, she realized how much easier the process could have been if her mother had made plans. There were so many things Sarah didn't know—what her mother would have wanted for her funeral, how she wanted to be cared for as her health declined, and where to find important documents. It was an emotional and logistical challenge that compounded the grief Sarah was already feeling.

That experience changed Sarah's perspective on her own aging. She didn't want her children to go through the same confusion and stress she had faced. So, Sarah took the time to proactively plan. She created a will, organized her financial documents, and made sure her children knew where everything was. She also had the difficult but necessary conversations about her long-term care wishes and what she wanted for her end-of-life care. It wasn't easy to think about, but it gave Sarah peace of mind knowing her family wouldn't have to face the same struggles.

Conclusion:
Leaving a Legacy of Care

The journey of caring for an aging parent is filled with lessons—some hard, some beautiful. And while none of us can stop the aging process, we can prepare for it in ways that make it easier for the people we love. By taking the time to plan for your own aging, you're not just making practical decisions—you're giving your family the gift of clarity and peace of mind.

Your legacy doesn't just end with the life you've lived—it continues with the care and consideration you've put into planning for the future. And in doing so, you're ensuring that when the time comes, your loved ones can focus on what truly matters: spending time with you, sharing memories, and walking with you through life's final chapters, knowing that the path has already been laid out with love and intention.

Resources for Proactive Aging Planning

- **AARP - Legal Checklist for Caregivers**
  AARP offers a detailed checklist to help individuals prepare legal documents such as wills, powers of attorney, and advance directives.
  - » **Website:** https://www.aarp.org/caregiving/financial-legal/info-2020/caregivers-legal-checklist.html

- **National Institute on Aging - Advance Care Planning**
  The National Institute on Aging provides resources on advance care planning, including how to create a living will, appoint a healthcare proxy, and make decisions about future medical care.
  - » **Website:** https://www.nia.nih.gov/health/advance-care-planning

- **ElderLawAnswers - Legal and Financial Planning for Aging**
  ElderLawAnswers offers information on estate planning, advance directives, and other legal matters important for aging individuals.
  » **Website**: https://www.elderlawanswers.com

- **The Conversation Project - End-of-Life Conversations**
  The Conversation Project provides tools and resources to help people talk with their families about their wishes for end-of-life care.
  » **Website**: https://theconversationproject.org

- **Long-Term Care Insurance - American Association for Long-Term Care Insurance (AALTCI)**
  AALTCI offers information on purchasing long-term care insurance, comparing policies, and understanding the benefits.
  » **Website**: https://www.aaltci.org

- **BenefitsCheckUp by the National Council on Aging**
  BenefitsCheckUp helps seniors find federal, state, and local programs that provide financial assistance for long-term care and other senior services.
  » **Website**: https://www.benefitscheckup.org

- **The National Institute on Aging - Planning for Long-Term Care**
  The NIA offers comprehensive guidance on long-term care options, how to pay for care, and what to consider when planning for future health needs.
  » **Website**: https://www.nia.nih.gov/health/long-term-care

- **Genworth - Cost of Care Survey**
  Genworth's annual Cost of Care Survey provides comprehensive data on the costs of long-term care, including home care, assisted living, and nursing homes across the U.S. This resource can help families plan financially for future care needs.
  » **Website**: https://www.genworth.com/aging-and-you/finances/cost-of-care.html

- **American Bar Association - Estate Planning Resources**
  The ABA offers extensive resources to help individuals plan their estates, draft wills, and prepare legal documents such as trusts and powers of attorney.
  » **Website:** https://www.americanbar.org/groups/real_property_trust_estate/resources/estate_planning/

- **Medicare - Long-Term Care Information**
  Medicare provides information about what services it covers for seniors, particularly for short-term rehabilitation care. However, Medicare does not cover long-term care, so it's important to understand the coverage limits and consider other financial planning options.
  » **Website:** https://www.medicare.gov/coverage/long-term-care

- **National Academy of Elder Law Attorneys (NAELA)**
  NAELA provides resources to find elder law attorneys who specialize in legal issues affecting older adults, including estate planning, Medicaid eligibility, and long-term care planning.
  » **Website:** https://www.naela.org

- **Caring.com - Guide to Senior Living and Care Options**
  Caring.com offers a guide to various senior living options, including independent living, assisted living, and memory care. This resource provides information about costs, services, and how to select the best option for your needs.
  » **Website:** https://www.caring.com/senior-living/

- **Social Security Administration - Retirement and Survivor Benefits**
  The Social Security Administration offers information on retirement and survivor benefits, which can provide financial assistance for surviving spouses and dependent family members. Understanding

these benefits can help you plan financially for the future and for your loved ones.
  » **Website:** https://www.ssa.gov/benefits/survivors/

Caregiving and Support Resources:

- **Family Caregiver Alliance (FCA):**

Offers educational support and resources for caregivers.
  » **Website:** https://www.caregiver.org

- **AARP Caregiving Resource Center:**

Provides tools and advice for caregivers, including guides on financial and legal matters.
  » **Website:** https://www.aarp.org/caregiving

- **National Family Caregiver Support Program (NFCSP):**

A federally funded program offering counseling, training, and respite care to caregivers.
  » **Website:** https://acl.gov/programs/support-caregivers/national-family-caregiver-support-program

- **Caregiver Action Network (CAN):**

Free resources, peer networks, and tools for family caregivers.
  » **Website:** https://www.caregiveraction.org

Senior Living and Long-Term Care Resources:

- **Eldercare Locator:**

Connects older adults and caregivers with local services like home health care, transportation, and senior centers.
  » **Website:** https://eldercare.acl.gov

- **Aging Life Care Association (ALCA):**
A network of geriatric care managers who assist with care planning, coordination, and aging-related decisions.
    » **Website**: https://www.aginglifecare.org

- **National Institute on Aging (NIA):**
Offers extensive resources for senior care, home safety, and aging in place.
    » **Website:** https://www.nia.nih.gov

Financial Resources and Insurance:

- **Benefits Checkup by National Council on Aging (NCOA):**
A tool to check eligibility for over 2,000 benefit programs for seniors.
    » **Website**: https://www.benefitscheckup.org

- **Medicare Rights Center:**
Helps individuals understand Medicare and their rights.
    » **Website:** https://www.medicarerights.org

- **SHIP (State Health Insurance Assistance Program):**
Free counseling on Medicare, Medicaid, and long-term care insurance.
    » **Website:** https://www.shiphelp.org

- **RxAssist:**
Patient assistance programs to help cover medication costs.
    » **Website:** https://www.rxassist.org

- **Veterans Aid & Attendance Benefits:**
Provides financial assistance to veterans and surviving spouses for long-term care costs.

» **Website:** https://www.va.gov/pension/aid-attendance-housebound

End-of-Life Planning and Hospice Resources:

- **National Hospice and Palliative Care Organization (NHPCO):**
  Educational resources on hospice care and end-of-life planning.
  » **Website**: https://www.nhpco.org

- **Compassion & Choices:**
  Resources for end-of-life planning, hospice care, and legal rights.
  » **Website:** https://www.compassionandchoices.org

- **Five Wishes (Aging with Dignity):**
  A guide for individuals to express their personal, emotional, and medical wishes for end-of-life care.
  » **Website:** https://www.fivewishes.org

- **Hospice Foundation of America (HFA):**
  Information on hospice services and grief support.
  » **Website:** https://hospicefoundation.org

Memory Care and Dementia Resources:

- **Alzheimer's Association:**
  Resources for families and caregivers dealing with Alzheimer's and dementia.
  » **Website:** https://www.alz.org

- **Memory Care Directory - LeadingAge:**
  Find memory care communities tailored for individuals with cognitive impairment.
  » **Website:** https://www.leadingage.org

- **Dementia Care Resources by Mayo Clinic:**
  Guides on dementia care, symptoms, and treatment options.
  - » **Website:** https://www.mayoclinic.org/diseases-conditions/dementia/care-at-mayo-clinic/mac-20352024

Home Care and Safety Resources:

- **Home Care Association of America (HCAOA):**
  Directory of home care providers and services for seniors.
  - » **Website:** https://www.hcaoa.org

- **National Association for Home Care & Hospice (NAHC):**
  Information on home health care services and how to find providers.
  - » **Website:** https://www.nahc.org

- **Rebuilding Together:**
  Provides home repairs and modifications for low-income seniors.
  - » **Website:** https://rebuildingtogether.org

- **Meals on Wheels America:**
  Delivers meals to seniors who are homebound and need nutritional support.
  - » **Website:** https://www.mealsonwheelsamerica.org

Legal Resources and Elder Law:

- **National Academy of Elder Law Attorneys (NAELA):**
  Connects families with elder law attorneys specializing in Medicaid, estate planning, and elder rights.
  - » **Website:** https://www.naela.org

- **MyDirectives:**
  Online platform for creating and storing advance care planning documents.
  - » **Website:** https://mydirectives.com

- **POLST (Physician Orders for Life-Sustaining Treatment):**
  Documents preferences for end-of-life care in medical emergencies.
  - » **Website:** https://polst.org

Support for Caregivers Resources:

- **Lotsa Helping Hands:**
  An online platform that allows families and friends to coordinate caregiving tasks.
  - » **Website:** https://www.lotsahelpinghands.com

- **The Well Spouse Association:**
  Support network for caregivers caring for chronically ill spouses.
  - » **Website:** https://wellspouse.org

www.ingramcontent.com/pod-product-compliance
Lightning Source LLC
Chambersburg PA
CBHW070149100426
42743CB00013B/2857